The Top 1000 Doo-Wop Songs:
Collector's Edition

by Anthony J. Gribin
& Matthew M. Schiff

ttgPress

The Top 1000 Doo-Wop Songs: Collector's Edition

All Rights Reserved

Copyright © 2014 Anthony J. Gribin, Ph.D & Matthew M. Schiff, M.D.

ISBN-13: 58000097512715

ttgPress

This book is dedicated to the (mostly) unsung men and women, some of whom appear on the cover, who managed to deliver by radio, 45 r.p.m. record or theater show, the music we all have come to love.

See overleaf containing pictures and legend.

Louis Sylvani, Val Shively, Wayne Stierle, Jerry Greene, Slim Rose, Alan Fredericks, Don K. Reed, Porky Chedwick, Steve Propes

Norm N. Nite, Donn Fileti, Eddie Gries, Douglas "Jocko" Henderson, Hal Jackson, Tommy "Dr. Jive" Smalls, Jerry Blavat, Ronnie Italiano, Sandy Italiano

Christine Vitale, George "Hound Dog" Lorenz, Phil Groia, Charlie Horner, Dick Clark, Gus Gossert, Peter Tripp, "Murray the K" Kaufman, Clay Cole

Gordon Skadberg, Frank Gengaro, Casey Kasem, Wolfman Jack, Hy Lit, Harvey Holiday, Al "The Mayor of Bronzeville" Benson, Alan Freed, "Symphony Sid" Torin

Marv Goldberg, David Hinckley, Hunter Hancock, Art Laboe, Dick "Huggie Boy" Hugg, Zenas "Daddy" Sears, Dick Biondi, Danny Stiles, Tom Luciani

Sal Mondrone, Bobby Jay, Richard Stamz, Bobby Diskin, Ed Engel, George Lavatelli, Terry Stewart, Lou Rallo, Jared Weinstein

Table of Contents

Introduction

This book is aimed at collectors who don't have much to collect any more and who also appreciate doo-wop music.

When we were young, many of us got enjoyment out of putting stamps in an album, opening a new pack of baseball cards smelling of cheap bubble gum, going through a roll of pennies to hunt for a rare Lincoln cent or walking to the local music store to get the latest and greatest 45 r.p.m. record. Everyone had a "need list" or a "want list," whether written down or in their heads. Other generations have fallen prey to collecting LPs or CDs, Barbie or American Girl dolls, Pokemon or Magic cards, or even pogs and beanie babies.

The things we like to collect stay with us, and is generational. Sixty-somethings are unlikely to collect pogs or Magic cards, and thirty somethings unlikely to want to hunt down dusty 45 r.p.m. records. Not surprisingly, our allegiance to a genre of music operates the same way. The central year of the doo-wop era was 1957. If the average kid started tuning into music at around ten years old, that puts the average fan's birth year at roughly 1947, and his or her age at 66, as of 2013. Sixty-six year olds are as unlikely to listen to rap, as rap lovers are to listen to doo-wop.

Yet we feel that our doo-wop music is somehow special. Not just to us, but to generations of music lovers. Doo-wop was the first genre created *for* teens *by* teens. It was crafted with teenage input as composers and performers and, along with sports, was the first frontier of racial integration. It is also an innocent music, containing heartfelt emotions that deal with all the torturous stages of first love. It's lyrics speak of "earth angels," "adorable babies" and "nature's creation of love." It asks the questions "who wrote the Book of Love?" and "I wonder why I love you like I do?" More recent musics do not shy away from depravity, dealing with villainous heroes, bitches and "hoes." The fact that music from the 1950s and 1960s is still readily available and popular on car radios and internet sites implies that many people agree with us. But why should we "collect" it?

The need to collect something, if not inborn, is important to our psychological growth. Collecting helped to form one's identity as a young person. Having a complete or almost complete collection of anything felt good, was an accomplishment, and made us feel better about ourselves. Flipping cards (closest to the wall or heads/tails) honed rudimentary competitive skills and trading them developed business acumen.

As we mature, the need to collect changes. Perhaps from collecting Lincoln cents to amassing wealth. From spending hours carefully placing stamps in albums to making one-off, sometimes impulsive purchases of a new tool from Home Depot, an antique firearm at a gun show, a concert t-shirt or even old fixer-upper car. We have less time to spend on our hobbies and realize the importance of money, although some of these impulse buys can be very very costly.

Somehow while we were growing up, the world changed. Kids today don't share the hobbies of our own youth. In their spare time, they play video games, skype with each other on computers or text/tweet/talk to each other on smart phones. And these high-stimulation activities tend to become compelling if not addicting. Collect stamps? Borrrring. It's hard to convince a young person that stamp collecting is educational, teaching geography, history and culture, when all they have to do is type a few words into Google to obtain the same information in greater detail.

And if you're playing war games over the net against others who are trying to kill your avatar before you get theirs, you don't need to flip baseball cards to learn how to compete. If you can download your favorite songs one at a time from iTunes for a buck a pop, why would you need to collect actual records, which are harder to find, have poorer sound quality and occupy an awful lot more space?

The result of these generational preferences and the pervasiveness of electronics has resulted in a death spiral for collectibles. Stamp collecting is an example. The transition from actual letters to email, tweets and paying bills on line, means less of a need for stamps; the less need for stamps, the less interest in stamps, the fewer stamp collectors. Fewer stamp collectors, fewer stamp stores, fewer stamp collectors.

When more baseball cards were being printed, it led to a collapse in the card collector's market, which resulted in fewer card collectors. This was fueled by greed when new companies (e.g. Upper Deck in 1989) saw that the Topps company was making a fortune and wanted some of the action. Cards were overproduced, and hawked by store owners as "investments" which fed the greed of collectors. Eighty-one billion cards were produced one year in the early 1990s, over 300 cards per person living in the United States.[1] Just what every grandma needed. The bubble soon burst.

When combing the internet for articles on the price trends of collectibles (stamps, coins, baseball cards and old records), there were many similarities among the genres. First, collecting for anything but pleasure is dumb.[2] The only people that will make money are the middle men; the salesmen. Second, all the trends are down, that is stamps, coins, cards and records lose value over time. The only exceptions are the rarest of the rare specimens, as in a Mickey Mantle rookie card, or extremely scarce stamps or

---

[1] http://www.baseballnation.com/2013/2/2/3943618/topps-2013-baseball-cards-review

[2] http://www.baseballnation.com/2013/2/2/3943618/topps-2013-baseball-cards-review

gold coins. With these, you had better know what you're doing because the person that's selling it to you wants his or her cut. All others lose value because the fewer collectors there are, the less the mid-value objects are desired and prices go down.

A third factor is eBay which, on the surface would seem to allow for more collecting. Which it does, but now everyone can become specialized. For example, the senior author sought to collect versions of "Them There Eyes," a song written by his mother in 1930. Within a few years, he amassed approximately 500 versions, on CDs, vinyl and via iTunes. We're quite certain that no one else on the planet has a better collection of TTE than he does. Or wants to, since he's an only child. The value of that collection? Close to zero. Others can amass equally obscure specialized collections, but with very little competition for product, that means low prices.

So what is a mature collector to do if they'd like to collect something beside dust? Remember, collecting is a bad investment so this will not be something that will be a legacy for children or grandchildren. Hence it can't cost too much money. Also as we are aging (hopefully with grace) the activity needs to be relatively sedentary and not require too much physical agility. Sort of on the level of a TV remote, rather than a video game controller.

Here's a riddle for you... what do doo-wop music and Sherlock Holmes stories have in common? The body of stories that Sherlock appeared in is exactly four books and 56 short stories. No more, no less. People interested in Holmes have analyzed the hell out of this fixed body of work, annotating, dissecting and pontificating on the stories and the characters based on it.[3] Doo-wop is almost in the same boat. The music was created within a relatively fixed era (1948-1963), with few exceptions. As a

---

[3] See, for example: The Annotated Sherlock Holmes: The Four Novels and Fifty-Six Short Stories Complete by Sir Arthur Conan Doyle and William S. Baring-Gould. Wings Books: 1992.

result, revivalists have done their own versions of the old tunes, since new material is not very welcome among audiences for doo-wop ("Looking For an Echo" by Kenny Vance & the Planetones and "Morse Code of Love" by the Capris are some of those few exceptions). So if you "study" or collect the songs of the era, you can be pretty sure that there won't be many new ones to chase down. It's nice to have a target that doesn't move, although golfers might argue with this thought.

A final requirement is that it has to interest us, but not necessarily anyone else. It is likely that something allied with our youth will fill the bill, but something that we can still appreciate. We think we've found the answer... doo-wop music. But not actual vinyl records or CDs, simply the tracks of the best sounds of the era. "Instead of spending years slowly building up a record collection through a significant amount of searching and purchasing, you could easily have the same records as a seasoned collector in however long it took you to type artist names and record titles into Google. As physical media collections gave way to digital media collections, the idea of a 'record collection'—which once implied work, as in actually going to obscure record stores and searching for and buying physical discs—started to fade away."[4]

Where do we get those tracks? Download them, one at a time, from record providers such as iTunes, hear them on a service such as YouTube since virtually all of our favorites are there, and find them in your basement on your old 45s, LPs, cassettes and CDs. We'll provide the "want list."

In this spirit, we present, "The Top 1000 Doo-Wop Songs: Collector's Edition."

---

[4] http://brittanytodd.hubpages.com/hub/The-Decrease-in-Value-of-Vinyl-Records

What Is Doo-Wop Music?

The reader might ask, "What makes doo-wop more important than other genres of music, say big band, British rock, heavy metal, grunge or alternative?" While all of these types of music will have nostalgia value for those who grew up with them, doo-wop sets itself apart psychologically.

Both authors are mental health professionals and are aware of the characteristics of adults who are happy as they become mature. For example, we all value love and relationships. We all seek to be happy in our lives and find pastimes that are familiar and soothing as a respite from our stress-laden lives. We all like things to be predictable and we strive for closure; that is, we don't like unfinished business. We also value getting along, living in harmony and mellowing out as the years pass. Doo-wop lets us do these things better than other types of music.

While all genres will provide fond memories of youth and young love to a middle aged (or older) person, doo-wop deals *exclusively* with young love as its subject matter. Exceptions are rare. Doo-wop is basically a happy, innocent music. There is little discord either in the lyrics or the melodies. Most doo-wops make you smile. Not think deeply or support a cause, just smile and maybe sing along.

The melodies, with their four-chord progressions, *always* seem familiar and soothing. In a way, that's a knock against the music; that it is too repetitive in its melodies and its "to be my guide/be my bride" lyrics. But along with repetition comes familiarity and comfort. We *know* these songs in our gut; we can often start humming one and end up singing another. Because many of them are similar, they blend.

Finally, the blending of voices that produces the harmony of doo-wop is a parable for the rest of life. Just as the singers blend and work together, so do we strive to "go along to get along." We now turn to the characteristics of the music we love.

The doo-wop style requires that there be at least three people singing. Two people don't count even when the arrangement sounds doo-woppy, as in songs by Marvin & Johnny, Johnny & Joe, Robert & Johnny and Don & Juan. We call that "duo-wop." There are also songs that sound doo-woppy performed by single artists, such as "Angel Baby" by Rosie & the Originals and "Love You So" by Ron Holden & the Thunderbirds. The songs have a doo-wop feel, tempo and doo-wop-friendly group name, but there's no vocal group. That's "uni-wop." For those of you who think we are taking our subject lightly, you are correct. This is a fun music and we intend to enjoy it thoroughly whether writing about or listening to it.

The usual group is comprised of four members, but five is common (three and six less so). Aside from the lead in a quartet, usually a tenor, a second tenor and baritone blend to produce background harmony, and there is a bass voice that either joins the harmonizers or sings a separate bass line under the harmony. When five are present, there are three harmonizers, a lead and a bass. Sometimes a tenor will float above the lead in falsetto.

Another characteristic of doo-wop, present more often than not, is the presence of nonsense syllables, such as "bon bon," bum bah bum," "tra la la" or "doo-wop." They are usually uttered by the bass, but can be sung by the harmonizers as well. Their frequency of use increased as the doo-wop era unfurled, to the point where their presence often became the focus of the song at the end of the era (examples are "Blue Moon" by the Marcels and most uptempo songs by the Earls).

Other common features of the genre are simple music and lyrics ("to be my guide/bride" rhymes), and light instrumentation except during the bridge (middle) of the song, when a sax often wails or a piano tinkles. The subject matter is almost invariably about young love, lost, found or desired from afar. It is a happy, joyful, harmonic and youthful music produced by a culture in relative harmony. It is a music by young people for young people and does not deal with the hardships of life as would the musics of later eras.

We've divided the era, which spans roughly 1948 to 1963, into three parts. "Paleo-Doo-Wop" runs from 1948 to 1954. Almost all of these early songs are by black groups. White singers hadn't entered the picture yet. Paleo- songs featured plaintive, sometimes operatic leads featuring soulful voices that often got their start singing gospel in church. The nonsense syllables employed were simple and infrequent (doh doh doh) The groups were comprised of older, more mature singers and sometimes the lyrics were lascivious ("It Ain't the Meat" by the Swallows and "Sixty Minute Man" by the Dominoes).

The Classical-Doo-Wop era (1955-1959) saw the entry of very young teens to the fray (Frankie Lymon, Pearl McKinnon) featuring high tenor "schoolboy" leads in 1955. A few years later white groups made the charts beginning with the white led, mixed race groups such as the Crests and Norman Fox & the Rob Roys, and then all-white groups like Danny & the Juniors, the Elegants and Dion & the Belmonts. Melodies and lyrics were simple and innocent, and nonsense syllables more pronounced. Falsetto was common, often used as a trail-off at the end of the song, and the bass line became more prominent.

The third period, Neo-Doo-Wop ran roughly from 1960-1963. This was the era of the "Oldies But Goodies" sound, that brought the old slow sounds to a new generation of teens. Being young, this new generation was attracted to glitzy exaggerations of the fast Classical sound. The bassi and falsetti were prominent, often leading a song, which didn't occur often in the Classical time frame. Old slow songs were remade uptempo (e.g. "Blue Moon," "Life Is But A Dream" and "The Closer You Are"). Tin Pan Alley composers joined the mix and instrumentation increased. A chart describing doo-wop characteristics through the years follows:

Doo-Wop Characteristics in Different Time Periods

	Pre-DW (before '48)	Paleo-DW ('48-'54)	Classical DW ('55-'59)	Neo-DW ('60-'63)	Post-DW (after '63)
Non-sense Sylls.	not present or used in different ways	emergence blow harmonies & simple patterns of non. sylls.	more complex patterns in almost every song	subdued in some cases and more complex patterns in others	words replace non. sylls. as background responses
Harmony Part	humming very much in background	given more voice may alternate with lead	given even more voice	same as classical	recedes into background
Falsetto	occasionally present but has operatic quality	present more often occasionally leads, operatic quality	almost always present, frequently leads, almost always used as trail-off	not always present but more freq. leads when present, used less as trail-off	diminished presence, almost never leads or used as trail-off
Bass	freq. bass leads and talking bridges, but not between stanzas not distinct from harmony	begins to separate from harmony, begins to punctuate stanzas	frequently introduces song, almost always separate from harmony by punctuating or riffing	same as classical, but sometimes used in exaggerated ways	used less as separate voice throughout
Beat	allied with jazz, r&b or other earlier styles	very little jazz influence, more allied with r&b	beat heavy & distinct (on 2nd & 4th beats), allied with rock & roll	same as classical except for pop-DW where beat is softer	remains heavy in most new musics

	Pre-DW (before '48)	Paleo-DW ('48-'54)	Classical DW ('55-'59)	Neo-DW ('60-'63)	Post-DW (after '63)
Instru-ments	heavier than standard doo-wop fare	less present than before, honky-tonk piano or organ typical	instruments unimportant except during break in mid-dle of song	instruments re-emerging	instruments much more important
Melody	blues or jazz progressions	melodies begin to simplify	simple melodies & four-chord structures common	more variation than in classical	significantly more variation in melodies
Lyrics	often lascivious in r&b, else mature love themes	still lascivious but innocent love themes begin to take over	almost exclusively innocent love, almost no politi-cizing or social commentary	lyrics remain innocent	most lyrics still deal with love, but social com-mentary & politicizing appears

The Historical Antecedents of Doo-Wop Music

Vocal group music has been around forever. We have records of sheet music written for quartets going back well over a century and vocal groups were recorded on discs and cylinders as soon as they were invented around 1890. Almost any and all non-classical music somehow influenced our music. It was born out of the confluence of gospel, popular music, barbershop, jazz, blues and rhythm and blues. The best source of detailed information on this evolution can be found in "The Encyclopedia of Early Vocal Groups: 1850-1950." [5]

Each of these musics, in turn, had its own set of ancestors. For example, the nonsense syllable of doo-wop can be traced to the imitation of instruments by the Mills Brothers in the 1930s, who in turn copied the sounds of the rhythm and horn sections of the big band sound. Background harmonies found in doo-wop can be traced to black gospel, which in turn combines white church music and Negro field chants (that came from Europe and Africa respectively). Rhythm in doo-wop can be traced back to post-war R&B, jazz, boogie woogie and swing. The AAB format of many uptempo doo-wops (especially early ones) comes from inner city and Mississippi blues. The pop-doo-wop style of the Platters is descended from the ballad style os the Ink Spots, which in turn comes from the early barbershop quartets of the earlier part of the twentieth century. The further we look back, the murkier it gets.

The social and political realities of the times must also be taken into account. For example, the further back in time we go, the slower music (and everything else)

---

[5] Friedman, Douglas & Gribin, Anthony. HarmonySongs, 2013.

changed and evolved. There were no radio or TV sets in the 1890s, and the recording of music had just begun. The most important medium for the performance of music was live entertainment. In the early 1900s only a small percentage of Americans had machines on which to play cylinders or records. People heard music at minstrel shows, concerts and houses of worship. One heard mainly local music, especially in rural areas. Faster evolution of musical styles couldn't occur until radio became commonplace, which allowed people to hear music from different parts of the country.

Another fact of life engrained in the evolution of music is segregation. Whites and blacks lived parallel, unequal lives in the years before the doo-wop era. Communication between the races and cross-fertilization of music was more difficult the further back we go, but it was helped by the tendency of musicians to be more liberal than the society as a whole, and by radio. Blacks and whites found it difficult to sing together (there are exceptions) and couldn't dance together in public, but could easily listen to each other's output over the ether.

Before the Classical Doo-Wop era, there were separate charts for white and black music, separate avenues for music publishing (ASCAP for white composers, BMI for black), and separate radio stations proffering black or white music. What broke down barriers were deejays such as Alan Freed, who brought black music to white audiences, and the entry of post-war youth into the fray. There were attempts to maintain segregation in music which petered out after a few years in the 1950s. Examples are cover records, whereby a black group would release a song which was copied and released (usually less well) by a white group and political railing against the ruination of white youth who were exposed to black culture. By 1960, the horse was out of the barn, and black music became the the property of all teenagers. The "Oldies But Goodies" series in 1961 brought black music to white teenagers, many for the first time.

Luckily, with the advent of the internet, we have almost unfettered access to all songs recorded earlier that influenced the doo-wop era. Past recordings can be bought on CDs or heard on your computer through the auspices of YouTube or sites devoted to early sounds. Google is a big help here. Just put a group, say the Boswell Sisters, in that search engine and information about them and music by them is instantly available. We've assembled a list of 100 Top Songs performed by vocal groups that preceded the doo-wop era. Some of the songs may be totally unfamiliar to doo-wop fans, but these are the sounds that led to the music we love.

We begin our list in 1930. Electrical (as opposed to mechanical) recording of sound began around 1925, and most of the vocal groups around at the time had high-pitched, formal voices which came through well when recorded mechanically, but sounded old fashioned and tinny over state of the art recording equipment. In 1930, the Rhythm Boys and Boswell Sisters roamed the airwaves, presenting a modern, jazzy sound that paved the way to the future of vocal group singing.

The list includes some songs from the late 1940s and early 1950s. These are not doo-wops, but may well have influenced the singers of the doo-wop era. The best and most complete source of information about these early vocal group recordings can be found in "The Encyclopedia of Vocal Group Harmony: 1850-1950" by Friedman and Gribin.

Top 100 Vocal Group Songs from Before the Doo-Wop Era

Crosby, Bing (w/Rhythm Boys)	Them There Eyes	1930
Boswell Sisters	When I Take My Sugar To Tea	1931
Mills Brothers	Tiger Rag	1931

Mills Brothers	Rockin' Chair	1932
Rollin' Smith's Rascals	Kickin' The Gong Around	1932
Three Keys	Wah Dee-Dah	1932
Five Spirits Of Rhythm	I Got Rhythm	1933
Mills Brothers	Jungle Fever	1934
Boswell Sisters	The Object Of My Affection	1935
Boswell Sisters	Alexander's Ragtime Band	1935
Four Blackbirds	Black-Eyed Susan Brown	1935
Ink Spots	Swingin' On The Strings	1935
Ink Spots	If I Didn't Care	1939
Ink Spots	My Prayer	1939
Cats & the Fiddle	Killing Jive	1939
Cats & the Fiddle	I Miss You So	1940
Five Breezes	Minute And Hour Blues	1940
Golden Gate Quartet	Stormy Weather	1940
Ink Spots	Java Jive	1940
Lewis Bronzeville Five	Low Down Gal Blues	1940
Pied Pipers (with Frank Sinatra)	I'll Never Smile Again	1940
Andrews Sisters	The Shrine Of St. Cecilia	1941
Andrews Sisters	Boogie Woogie Bugle Boy	1941
Ink Spots	I Don't Want To Set The World On Fire	1941
Modernaires	Chattanoogo Choo Choo	1941
Andrews Sisters	Don't Sit Under The Apple Tree	1942
Dinning Sisters	The Way You Look Tonight	1943
Four Vagabonds	Rose Ann Of Charing Cross	1943
Mills Brothers	Paper Doll	1943
Song Spinners	Comin' In On A Wing And A Prayer	1943
Southern Sons	Praise The Lord And Pass The The Ammunition	1943
Fitzgerald, Ella (w/Ink Spots)	I'm Beginning To See The Light	1944

Five Red Caps	I've Learned A Lesson I'll Never Forget	1944
Merry Macs	Mairzy Doats	1944
Mills Brothers	Till Then	1944
Brown Dots	For Sentimental Reasons	1945
Four Dots	As Strange As It Seems	1945
Basin Street Boys	I Sold My Heart To The Junkman	1946
Cats 'N' Jammer Three	I Cover The Waterfront	1946
Cats 'N' Jammer Three	One Hundred Years From Today	1946
Charioteers	You Make Me Feel So Young	1946
Churchill, Savannah (bb the Sentimentalists)	I Want To Be Loved But Only By You	1946
Coleman Brothers	Get Away Mr. Satan, Get Away	1946
Delta Rhythm Boys	Just A-Sittin' And A-Rockin'	1946
Four Knights	Funny How You Get Along Without Me	1946
Four Tunes (aka Senimental-ists)	I'd Rather Be Safe Than Sorry	1946
Charioteers	Chi-Baba Chi-Baba	1947
Deep River Boys	Jealous	1947
Fitzgerald, Ella (w/Andy Love Quartet)	That's My Desire	1947
Four Vagabonds	The Gang That Sang Heart Of My Heart	1947
Four Vagabonds	P.S. I Love You	1947
Johnson, Bill (& His Musical Notes)	Dream Of A Lifetime	1947
Melody Masters	Don't You Ever Mind Them	1947
Scamps	I'll Never Smile Again	1947
Velvetones	It's Written All Over Your Face	1947
Churchill, Savannah (bb the Four Tunes)	The Best Of Friends	1948

Deep River Boys	Recess In Heaven	1948
Four Blues	It Takes A Long Tall Brown Skinned Gal	1948
Master Keys	Don't Cry Darling	1948
Radars	You Belong To Me	1948
Beavers	If You See Tears In My Eyes	1949
Blenders	I Can Dream, Can't I	1949
Cabineers	Whirlpool	1949
Charioteers	A Kiss And A Rose	1949
Delta Rhythm Boys	Fantastic	1949
Four Jacks	I Challenge Your Kiss	1949
James Quintet	Bewildered	1949
Johnson, Bill (& His Musical Notes)	I Love You More Each Day	1949
Red Caps (Steve Gibson & the)	Blueberry Hill	1949
Rhythm Masters	Until Now	1949
Skyscrapers (Browley Guy & the)	That Gal Of Mine	1949
Striders	Hesitating Fool	1949
Tom Cats	Honey I'm Yours	1949
Ames Brothers	Rag Mop	1950
Bachelors	Yesterday's Roses	1950
Bachelors	Hereafter	1950
Balladeers	I Never Knew I Loved You	1950
Brown, Ruth (bb the Delta Rhythm Boys)	Sentimental Journey	1950
Cap-Tans	I'm So Crazy For Love	1950
Cap-Tans	With All My Love	1950
Churchill, Savannah (bb the Striders)	Once There Lived A Fool	1950
Dozier Boys	Pretty Eyes	1950
Four Blues	As Long As I Live	1950

Jubilaires	A Dream Is A Wish Your Heart Makes	1950
Nichols, Ann (with the Bluebirds)	Let Me Know	1950
Palmer Brothers	Brown Boy	1950
Rivals	Don't Say You're Sorry Again	1950
Shadows	I'd Rather Be Wrong Than Blue	1950
Songmasters	What Do Your Tears Really Mean	1950
Striders	Cool Saturday Night	1950
Whispers	I've Got No Name	1950
Cabineers	Whirlpool	1951
James Quintet	A Neighborhood Affair	1951
King Odom Four	Teardrops Of Angels	1951
Mariners	They Call The Wind Mariah	1951
Sugartones	Today Is Your Birthday	1951
Varieteers	I'll Try To Forget I Loved You	1951
Williams, Billy (Quartet)	You Made Me Love You	1951
Comets (Herb Kenny & the)	When The Lights Go On Again	1952
Starr, Kay (bb the Lancers)	I Waited A Little Too Long	1952

Singers, Styles & Songs

We're not giving up our secrets yet. Before we present our Top 1000 records, we're going to present the reader with some other lists to think about, involving singers, groups, the songs themselves and other opinions about what the top tracks should be. We'll start off discussing lead singers and bass men, then turn to differing styles of doo-wop.

The Best Lead Singers

      Ronnie Italiano, President of the United in Group Harmony Association was on WNYE radio for twenty or so years. At some point early in 1995, he ran a contest to determine the best lead singer of all time. Ten leads were nominated by calls to his radio show, naming a singer and one song on which he sang lead. When two votes were received for a singer, he was "in" for the final 10. When two votes were recorded for one song, the song was "in." Each week, for five weeks, the 10 chosen singers were presented in pairs for a vote. Number 10 was paired against number nine, etc. Phoned-in ratings were limited by Italiano to between 80 and 100, since allowing a full range had resulted in lowballing in a previous contest. Ten ratings for each singer were tallied. The results are shown below:

10th	Lee Andrews	Hearts	940
9th	Maithe Marshall	Ravens	944
8th	Sonny Til	Orioles	962
7th	James Shepard	Heartbeats/ Limelights	963
6th	Bobby Lester	Moonglows	966.9
5th	Rudy West	Five Keys	976
4th	Clyde McPhatter	Dominoes/Drifters	979
1st (tie)	Solly McElroy	Flamingos/Moroccos	993
1st (tie)	Eugene Mumford	Larks/Dominoes	993
1st (tie)	Willie Winfield	Harptones	993

A run-off was held on Feb. 15, 1995. Solly McElroy, who unfortunately languished and died of cancer during the time these playoffs were held, finished third with a total of 985. Mumford and Winfield again tied however, with 989 points. In the second run-off three weeks later, Willie Winfield edged out Gene Mumford, 995 to 993, although Italiano admitted to eliminating some outlying scores from both sides.

Though most people who love this music would not quibble much with the choice of these ten singers as among the best, it is clear that the purists that contributed to Ronnie I's sample were clearly biased in favor of black soulful singers. This audience chose to omit some well-known leads like Fred Parris of the Five Satins, (Little) Anthony Gourdine of the Imperials, Dion DiMucci of the Belmonts and Johnny Maestro of the Crests. Apparently politics has insinuated itself into the very heart of the doo-wop world!

It is also unfortunate that Italiano did not employ more rigorous rating procedures to achieve his goal, since he ended up fudging the results in the end.

As a counterbalance to the UGHA take on lead singers, Ed Engel offered his preferences for the best white leads.[6] In alphabetical order, they were:

Nicky Addeo	Darchaes
Jimmy Beaumont	Skyliners
Jay Black	Americans
Larry Chance	Earls
Eddie Delmar	Bob Knight Four
Dion DiMucci	Belmonts
Teddy Graybill	Stardrifts, Concords
Jordan	Fascinations
Richard Kelly	Ovations

---

[6] Engel, Ed. "Top 20 White Lead Singers." Echoes Of The Past, Issue #4, Summer 1988, p. 22.

Mike Lasman	Utopians
Dennis Lowell	Explorers
Johnny Maestro	Crests
Anthony Maresca	Sophomores, Twilights, Dynamics
Carlo Mastrangelo	Belmonts
Tony Passalacqua	Fascinators
Vito Picone	Elegants
Joe Prolia	Fabulous Four, Five J's
Dominic Safuto	Randy & the Rainbows
Nick Santamaria	Capris
Jay Siegel	Tokens

Styles of Leads

To complete the discussion of lead singers, in "The Complete Book of Doo-Wop" we offered fifteen different categories of leads, which appear below:

Operatic

Time frame: Mid-1930s to late 1940s

Examples: Billy Williams (Charioteers), Bill Kenny (Ink Spots), Maithe Marshall and Joe Van Loan (Ravens).

Notes: High-register male voice anchored in the pre-doo-wop era. Affected and formal delivery geared to an adult audience. First used by Williams but made famous by Kenny, in a string of hits beginning in 1939 with "If I Didn't Care."

Jazzy

Time frame: Late 1940s

Examples: Jimmy Ricks (Ravens), Ormand Wilson (Basin Street Boys).

Notes: Romantic, adult and sophisticated.

Romantic

Time frame: Late 1940s through late 1950s

Examples: Sonny Til (Orioles), Willie Winfield (Harptones), later Eugene Mumford (Dominoes).

Notes: Til set the standard for romantic leads as a matinee idol on the chitlin circuit.

Gospel

Time Frame: Early 1950s through late 1950s

Examples: Clyde McPhatter (Dominoes, Drifters), Jackie Wilson (Dominoes), David Baughan (Checkers), early Eugene Mumford (Larks).

Notes: Wailing, crying, living, dying. Melismatic and, at times, ethereal. Call and response common between lead and background. Aimed at black audiences.

Bluesy

Time Frame: Early 1950s through late 1950s (eventually transitioned to soul).

Examples: Early Rudy West (Five Keys), Junior Denby (Swallows), Bobby Lester and Harvey Fuqua (Moonglows), Solly McElroy (Flamingos).

Notes: Moonglows and Flamingos influenced by Chicago blues. Denby sounds like he's sitting on a barroom stool. Rudy West on the borderline between blues and gospel.

Sweet/Cute

Time Frame: Early 1950s to mid-1950s

Examples: Eddie Rich (Swallows), Ray Wooten (Mellomoods), Joe Duncan (Vocaleers), George Grant (Castelles).

Notes: Young teens trying to sound romantic and adult-like before Frankie Lymon made it okay for a kid to sound like a kid. Thus the precursor to the schoolboy style lead. Typified by Bobby Robinson's Red Robin groups.

Pop

Time Frame: Mid- to late 1950s

Examples: Tony Williams (Platters), later Rudy West (Five Keys), Nate Nelson (Flamingos).

Notes: Generally refers to "blaccent"-free leads with good voices that would sell to a whte audience. The material these leads were given was generally geared for adults, although teens liked the songs too.

New York Style

Time Frame: 1953 to early 1960s

Examples: Sonny Norton (Crows), Herman Dunham and Milton Love (Solitaires), Earl Carroll (Cadillacs), Earl Lewis (Channels).

Notes: Pleading leads doing slow ballads, with heavy background, lots of riffing bass and falsetto. Dialectic and slangy.

Stylized

Time Frame: 1954 to early 1960s

Examples: James "Shep" Sheppard (Heartbeats, Limelites), Anthony Gourdine (Little Anthony & the Imperials), later Lee Andrews (Hearts).

Notes: Sounded as if they were acting out the lyrics as they sang them. Stilted yet effective way of sounding out the words.

Schoolboy

Time Frame: 1956 to end of era in 1960s

Examples: Frankie Lymon (Teenagers), Lewis Lymon (Teenchords), Pearl McKinnon (Kodaks).

Notes: Kids with high tenor voices, singing like kids. Earlier youngsters sang rather mournful ballads with adult themes and lyrics (see Sweet/Cute). This generation offered upbeat, uptempo songs with simple lyrics.

Gang

Time Frame: 1956 through 1959

Examples: Mack Starr (Paragons), Adam Jackson (Jesters), Ernest Harriston (Bopchords).

Notes: These guys get the job done without smoothness. Sound romantic yet you might prefer not to turn your back on them. Primarily a New York phenomenon.

Rock 'n' Roll

Time Frame: 1955 through the end of the era

Examples: Kripp Johnson (Dell Vikings), Herb Cox (Cleftones), Johnny Maestro (Crests), Norman Fox (Rob Roys), Danny Rapp (Danny & the Juniors).

Notes: More or less blaccent-free leads in a delivery that was aimed at a white teen audience. Heavy beat with greater reliance of instruments.

West Coast

Time Frame: Mid-1950s through late 1950s

Examples: Jesse Belvin (Cliques), Cleve Duncan (Penguins), Arthur Lee Maye (Crowns).

Notes: Generally laid-back vocal style compared to East Coasters. Short on diction, long on feeling.

White

Time Frame: 1958 through end of the era

Examples: Dion DiMucci (Belmonts), Jimmy Beaumont (Skyliners), Jimmy Gallagher (Passions), Larry Chance (Earls), Joey Canzano (Duprees).

Notes: Just as almost all black leads grew up with gospel, learning and practicing the art of melisma (many notes per syllable), many white singers grew up listening to opera or crooners like Sinatra, Crosby, Como and Bennett. Crooners avoid melisma, holding their notes for longer periods of time. Less "soulful" than black leads.

Falsetto

Time Frame: 1950 through the end of the era

Examples: Nolan Strong (Diablos), Julius McMichael (Paragons), Al Banks (Turbans), Earl Lewis (Channels).

Notes: Falsetto is primarily a technique that has been used by lead singers for part or all of the song (e.g. Little Joe Cook of the Thrillers on "Peanuts" and "Lilly Lou"), by lead singers who convert from tenor in the trail off at the end of the song (e.g. Norman Fox of the Rob Roys in "Tell My Why"), by second leads usually during the bridge (Al Crump of the Heartbeats on "Tormented"), as an echo to the lead (in "Dear Lord" by the Continentals), or by a first tenor behind the lead during choruses (Billy Taylor of the Castelles on "Marcella").

Singers have used falsetto leads throughout the entire doo-wop era; from Buddy Bailey of the Clovers in "Yes Sir, That's My Baby" in 1950 to Julius McMichael of the Paragons on "Florence" in 1957 to Frank Mancuso of the Imaginations on the white-style doo-wop "Hey You" from 1961. Thus falsetto crosses both time and color boundaries throughout the doo-wop years.

Use of multiple falsettos is found occasionally. "Alone" by the Universals (1957) has a falsetto lead with a falsetto tenor behind the lead, as does "House Of Love" (1958) by Henry Hall and the Five Bellaires and "Queen of the Angels" by the Orients (1964), while "Plan For Love," and early effort by the Flamingos, features shrill double falsettos backing up the lead tenor.

The Best Bass Men

     Aside from the lead singer of a doo-wop vocal group, the singer of most interest, fun and centrality to how this genre is recognized is the bass voice. Who can possibly forget...

> "Dun dun dun,
> Duh dun duh dun dun,
> Duh duh dun dun dun,
> Duh dun, duh duh duh duh duh duh duh..."[7]

Or,   "Sha duh dah dah,
       Sha duh dah duh dah duh, bah doo... (4 times)
       Ah, dyip dyip dyip dyip dyip dyip dyip dyip
       Bum mum mum mum mum mum..."[8]

     One might argue that without a distinct bass voice spouting wonderful catchy nonsense syllables, there would be no such thing as doo-wop. That all groups would sound like the Four Preps or the Four Freshmen. Not that these guys were bad. On the contrary, they were the best of their ilk, but they were not a lot of fun for the doo-wop generation. They represented the vocal group music aimed at white adults. The cover records of the mid- to late 1950s demonstrates this. If a black group came out with a catchy tune, say "Earth Angel" by the Penguins, within a couple of weeks a white pop group (in this case the Crew Cuts) would come out with a "cover record." The major record label that released the cover would make money without much expense or risk and the world would be safe

---

[7] From "I Wonder Why" by Dion & the Belmonts. Bass is Carlo Mastrangelo.

[8] From "Get A Job" by the Silhouettes. Bass is Raymond Edwards.

from black music which, as we all know, was ruining the minds of white youth.

So who were the best bass men? As was done for lead singers, Ronnie Italiano ran a contest to see who was the top banana in bassland.[9] He picked ten bassmen on his own, limiting the menu to those guys who sang both harmony and lead parts. This eliminated riffers like Charles Moffit of the Velours and Fred Johnson of the Marcels. It also reflected his preference for earlier sounds, since recordings later in the doo-wop era did not often feature bass leads.

He played sample songs and asked the first ten callers from his audience to rate them by choosing a number between 80 and 100 (the range was limited because he was afraid some voters would "low ball" some entrants. The nominees and results were:

10th	Norris "Bunky" Mack	Swallows	927
9th	Will "Dub" Jones	Cadets/Jacks	934
8th	Steve Gibson	Red Caps	956
7th	David McNeil	Larks/Dominoes	972
6th	Bill Brown	Dominoes/Checkers	975
5th	Lee Gaines	Delta Rhythm Boys	979
4th	Bobby Nunn	Robins/Coasters	983
3rd	Tommy Evans	Ravens/Drifters	989
2nd	Jimmy Ricks	Ravens	996
1st	Gerald Gregory	Spaniels	997

The results surprised even Mr. Italiano. He had a hard time believing that Jimmy Ricks didn't win, even though he held Gerald Gregory in high esteem. Apparently, a bass injustice occurred. Other noteworthy bass leads left out of this competition were Bill Pinckney of the Drifters,

---

[9] In March, 1995 on "The R&B Party," his Wednesday night radio show on WNYE in Brooklyn, NY.

Bob Karnegay of the Du Droppers and Harold Winley of the Clovers.

The Best Riffers

The bassi included in the competition sang during the early years of doo-wop. Later bassmen riffed and were "power basses" and rarely sang lead. In our opinion, the Ten Best were, in alphabetical order:

Fred Barksdale/Pat Gaston	Solitaires
Sherman Garnes	Teenagers
Gerald Gregory	Spaniels
Andrew Johnson/John Russell/Charles Di Bella	Five Discs
Fred Johnson	Marcels
Carlo Mastrangelo	Belmonts
Leroy McNeil	Nutmegs
Charles Moffet	Velours
Wally Roker	Heartbeats
Alex Miranda	Eternals

The reader will notice that Gerald Gregory is the only bass to appear on both lists, bridging the gap between two generations of bassmen and displaying a versatility not often seen.

The result of these riffers were classical and neo-doo-wop gems that represent the doo-wop style in the minds of many aficionados. To complete our bass-ic list, here are thirty songs with great contributions from bass voices, alphabetized by group:

Bosstones	Mope-Itty-Mope
Contenders	The Clock
Delroys	Bermuda Shorts

DeMilles	Donna Lee
Deltas	Lamplight
Devotions	Rip Van Winkle
Dion & the Belmonts	I Wonder Why
Du Mauriers	All Nite Long
Eternals	Babalu's Wedding Day
Five Discs	Never Let You Go
Flips, Little Joey & the	Bongo Stomp
Green, Barbara & group	Long Tall Sally
Halos	Nag
Lee, Curtis (backed by the Halos)	Pretty Little Angel Eyes
Magnificents	Up On The Mountain
Magnificent Four	The Closer You Are
Marcels	Blue Moon
Mayer, Nathaniel/Fabulous Twilights	Village Of Love
Monotones	Book Of Love
Nutmegs	Let Me Tell You
Quotations	Imagination
Poets	Vowels Of Love
Rivingtons	Papa Oom-Mow-Mow
Silhouettes	Get A Job
Solitaires	Walking Along
Summits	Go Back Where You Came From
Temptations	Roaches
Velours	Can I Come Over Tonight
Vito & the Salutations	Unchained Melody
Whirlwinds	Heartbeat

Sub-Styles of Doo-Wop

Within the doo-wop genre there were different kinds of sounds, distinct from one another, that warrant further attention. They are Schoolboy Doo-Wop, Gang-Doo-Wop, Pop Doo-Wop, the White Group Sound and the Girl Group Sound.

Schoolboy Doo-Wop

We'll turn first to the "schoolboy" sound, which emerged around 1956. As thirteen year olds heard the "older" guys flinging their doo-wops at subway walls, they formed their own groups and started singing. While groups comprised of young teens, such as Ray "Buddy" Wooten and his Mello-Moods, were around since the early 1950s, they sang adult themes, geared to adult audiences though they sounded like the kids they were. "Where Are You" and "How Could You," were beautiful and serious ballads about being ditched by a woman, and were a far cry from the innocence contained in the offerings of the Teenagers and Teenchords a few years later. A second youthful group of this type was Philadelphia's Castelles, led by George Grant, who put out a string of beautiful ballads, again with adult themes, such as "Over A Cup of Coffee," "My Girl Awaits Me," "This Silver Ring" and "Heavenly Father."

Authentic schoolboy doo-wops hit the airwaves in early 1956, led by "Why Do Fools Fall in Love" by Frankie Lymon and the Teenagers, although the Leslie Martin-led Schoolboys, with the two-sided hit "Please Say You Want Me/Shirley" and the Cubs, with "I Hear Wedding Bells" preceded them by a few months. The defining characteristic of this sub-style is the high tenor lead (or "castrato") of a male or female in their early teenage years. Frankie Lymon was the most well-known singer in this category and arguably of the entire doo-wop era. He and his group, the Teenagers, met with the most commercial success as well.

Many good leads singers, like Frankie's brother Lewis Lymon with his Teenchords and Leslie Martin (Schoolboys) followed in Frankie's footsteps, but never could fill his shoes. Words and music in this substyle were even more simple and predictable than in the average classical doo-wop offering. The appeal lay in the catchiness of the tunes and novelty of the sound. Notable female leads in this group include Pearl McKinnon (Kodaks, "Little Boy and Girl/ Teenager's Dream"), Pat Cordel (Crescents, "Darling Come Back") and June Bateman (Marquis, "Bohemian Daddy").

Here are our picks for the ten best:

Desires	Let It Please Be You
Elchords	Peppermint Stick
Hemlocks (Little Bobby Rivera &)	Cora Lee
Kodaks	Little Boy And Girl
Schoolboys	Please Say You Want Me
Students	I'm So Young
Teenagers (Frankie Lymon &)	Why Do Fools Fall In
Teenchords (Lewis Lymon &)	I'm So Happy
Tops (Little Jimmy Rivers &)	Puppy Love
Valchords	Candy Store Love

Gang Doo-Wop

Doo-wop evolved in urban areas that fostered toughness, bravado and competitiveness. Social life for teens centered around local gangs, community centers and playgrounds. Singing groups, which often developed from within these gangs or clubs, would engage in "singing rumbles," or talent contests which were held at local parks or community centers. As one might imagine, the audiences were usually partisan and enthusiastic at these events, which were often stepping-stones to a recording studio, either because a music professional was scouting the talent or the prize for winning was a chance to record.

The prototypical album, "The Paragons Meet The Jesters," is a figurative extension of these singing rumbles. The album cover features two tough-looking teens sporting the latest in gang attire. These groups often came from Harlem or Brooklyn in New York City. Phil Groia, an expert on these groups, further narrows down their turf to between 115th and 119th streets, and between 5th and 8th avenues in Manhattan (e.g. the Matadors, Jesters, Bop-Chords and Love Notes).[10]

In the days before the equality of the sexes guys had to appear cocky and talk brashly. This posturing and braggadocio when applied to doo-wop created the Gang substyle. The harmonies in this style were intricate, using much bass and falsetto. Falsetto leads were common as well. The end products sounded rough and had pounding beats surrounding catchy melodies. Our Top Ten are:

---

[10] Groia, Phil. They All Sang On The Corner. Port Jefferson, N.Y.: Phillie Dee Enterprises, 1983.

Bop Chords	Castle In The Sky
Cadillacs	Speedoo
Channels	That's My Desire
Charts	Zoop
Continentals	Dear Lord
Jesters	I'm Falling In Love
Love Notes	United
Matadors	Vengeance
Paragons	The Vows Of Love
Whirlers	Tonight And Forever

Pop Doo-Wop

Gang Doo-Wop came directly from the streets. At other times, the sound was molded by record company executives whose job it was to sell records. Looking for commercial success, many label owners turned to the "prep" sound of the Four Lads, Preps, Aces and Freshmen. These groups were influenced by the pop groups of the 1940s, like the Ink Spots, Mills Brothers, Modernaires and Pied Pipers. They harmonized beautifully, but met few other doo-wop criteria.

The strategies to blend this preppy sound with the teen-oriented doo-wop style were to issue "cover" records (wherein a white group would record/release a hit record by a black group), the softening of the doo-wop style so it would appeal to a wider age range, and jazzing up the "old standards" so that they would be fresh for the younger generation. We have called the outgrowth of these collective strategies "Pop Doo-Wop." Arrangers would mute or eliminate doo-wop characteristics so that falsetto was rarely used, bass singers blended with the harmonizers rather than standing alone and nonsense syllables were simpler, softer and sometimes absent. The result was that songs ended up being somewhere between the doo-wop and prep styles. Our Top Ten follows:

Avalons	My Heart's Desire
Castells	So This Is Love
Duprees	You Belong To Me
Echoes	Baby Blue
Fidelitys	The Things I Love
Fleetwoods	Come Softly To Me
Jaguars	The Way You Look Tonight
Platters	My Prayer
Skyliners	Pennies From Heaven
Tymes	So Much In Love

The White Group Sound

Since early black doo-wop and rhythm and blues was almost invisible to white teens in the early 1950s, white teens were invisible as creators of doo-wop music until schoolboy doo-wop groups hit the market in the mid-1950s. Because whites and blacks lived separately, the cross-fertilization of music from blacks to whites was slower than that between blacks and other blacks. Black kids heard other kids singing just about every day, in the playgrounds, school hallways or local social clubs. Whites got their music from the radio and churches.

Further, the church music that black teens heard was soulful, melismatic, call-and-response gospel. White kids heard hymnal music in church, and crooners, such as Sinatra or Crosby, at home. Both were a lot further away from doo-wop than what their black counterparts heard. Net-net: they got a late start.

The floodgates opened in 1958, starting with "I Wonder Why" by Dion & the Belmonts who instantly became household names. "The group had a real flair for arrangements - what attracted me to them instantly was their first biggie, "I Wonder Why" with the voices chiming in one at a time. I almost ruined my vocal chores trying to sing all three parts at once, and trying to imitate Dion's teen-age nasality... I think every kid in my school idolized Dion & the Belmonts when the group was hot."[11]

The White Group Sound, a substyle of doo-wop, can itself be subdivided into four mostly (but not totally) distinct subgroups that existed side by side. The first was the hard doo-wop style that usually featured a power bass that came on the scene after "I Wonder Why." The second was the rock 'n' roll oriented sound represented by Danny & the Juniors. The third was a soft doo-wop sound exemplified by "Little Star" (Elegants) and "Hushabye" (Mystics). And the last was the Pop Doo-Wop style discussed before. Fifteen Top Hits for each of the four categories is listed below, omitting girl groups because they are talked about in the next section.

---

[11] Ward, Ed. "Italo-American Rock." In Miller, Jim, Ed., The Rolling Stone Illustrated History Of Rock & Roll, New York: Rolling Stone Press, 1980.

Power Bass

Arrogants	Mirror Mirror
DeMilles	Donna Lee
Devotions	Rip Van Winkle
Dion & the Belmonts	I Wonder Why
Earls	Remember Then
Encounters	Don't Stop
Eternals	Babalu's Wedding Day
Excellents	You Baby You
Five Discs	Adios
Four J's	Here Am I Broken Hearted
Quotations	Ala-Men-Sa-Aye
Selections	Guardian Angel
Tokens	Tonight I Fell In Love
Treblechords	Theresa
Salutations, Vito & the	Unchained Melody

Rock 'n' Roll

Bell Notes	I've Had It
Original Casuals	So Tough
Danny & the Juniors	At The Hop
Danny & the Juniors	Rock And Roll Is Here To Stay

Del Satins	Teardrops Follow Me
Diamonds	The Stroll
Dion (bb the Del Satins)	Runaround Sue
Dovells	Bristol Stomp
Dovells	No No No
Nino & the Ebbtides	Juke Box Saturday Night
Nicky & the Nobles	Poor Rock 'n' Roll
Reflections	Just Like Romeo And Juliet
Regents	Barbara Ann
Rockin' Chairs	Memories Of Love
Royal Teens	Short Shorts

Soft Doo-Wop

Bob Knight Four	Good Goodbye
Caslons	Anniversary of Love
Chaperones	Cruise To The Moon
Dennis & the Explorers	Vision Of Love
Echoes	Baby Blue
Elegants	Little Star
Emotions	Echo
Fascinators	Who Do You Think You Are
Fleetwoods	Mr. Blue
Imaginations	Hey You

Mello-Kings	Tonite Tonite
Mystics	Hushabye
Passions	I Only Want You
Randy & the Rainbows	Denise
Safaris	Image Of A Girl

Pop Doo-Wop

Castells	So This Is Love
Chimes	Once In A While
Classics	Till Then
Demensions	Over The Rainbow
Dion & the Belmonts	Where Or When
Duprees	My Own True Love
Duprees	Why Don't You Believe Me
Roomates	Band Of Gold
Royal Teens	Believe Me
Skyliners	Lonely Way
Skyliners	This I Swear
Tempos	See You In September
Temptations	Barbara
Three Chuckles	Runaround
Three Friends	Blanche

The Girl Group Sound

Women weren't much of a factor until the end of the doo-wop era; the early 1960s. Guys hung out and formed singing groups on the streets and playgrounds, girls generally didn't "hang out." When girl groups formed, it was usually in school under the tutelage of a music teacher who ran the chorus. Thus there might be one girl group inside a school and ten guy groups singing in the immediate vicinity of that school. Many more male groups sang and recorded than female groups. So just as white groups got a late start compared to black groups, so did girl groups start later than guy groups.

There was also a belief on the part of record company execs that since women bought the records, they would be more interested in the output of male groups. Girl groups were innocent, unlike the worldly seductive single artists such as Lady Day, Lena Horne, Sarah Vaughan and Savannah Churchill. And the wide range of male voice parts in doo-wop was new, while the blended harmonies of female groups had been around for decades. The Andrews Sisters, McGuire Sisters, Chordettes and Fontaine Sisters didn't sound all that different to the untrained ear.

So, for the purpose of recommending songs of note, we've broken female contributions into two flavors: female leads fronting male groups and all-female groups. Female-fronting-male-groups were closer to R&B than they were to doo-wop. As stated, there weren't many early girl-only groups and the female leads were definitely women, not girls.

Ten Best R&B Songs: Female Lead with Male Group, 1948-1954

Ella Fitzgerald/Delta Rhythm Boys	Paper Moon (1945)
Savanna Churchill/Sentamentalists	I Want To Be Loved (But Only By You) (1946)
Ella Fitzgerald/Andy Love Quartet	That's My Desire (1947)
Savannah Churchill/Five Kings	Let's Call A Spade A Spade (1947)
Savannah Churchill/Four Tunes	Time Out For Tears (1948)
Little Esther/Robins	Double Crossin' Blues (1950)
Ruth Brown/Delta Rhythm Boys	Sentimental Journey (1950)
Dinah Washington/Ravens	Out In The Cold Again (1951)
Little Esther/Dominoes	Heart To Heart (1951)
Viola Watkins/Crows	Seven Lonely Days (1953)

Twenty Best Doo-Wop Songs: Female Lead with Male Group, 1954-1957

By 1954, a more youthful sound and younger singers began to prevail. Doo-wop characteristics were provided by the male background singers.

Capris	God Only Knows (1954)
Charmers	The Beating Of My Heart (1954)
Mellows (Lillian Leach & the)	How Sentimental Can I Be (1954)
Cole, Ann (with the Suburbans)	Are You Satisfied (1955)
Mellows (Lillian Leach & the)	Yesterday's Memories (1955)
Mellows (Lillian Leach & the)	Smoke From Your Cigarette (1955)
Chestnuts	Love Is True (1956)
Crescents (Pat Cordel & the)	Darling Come Back (1956)
Marquis	Bohemian Daddy (1956)
McFadden, Ruth (with the Supremes)	Darling, Listen To The Words Of This Song (1956)
McFadden, Ruth (with the Royaltones)	Two In Love (With One Heart) (1956)
McFadden, Ruth (with the Harptones)	School Boy (1956)
Mellows (Lillian Leach & the)	My Darling (1956)

Sensations	Yes Sir, That's My Baby (1956)
Sensations	Please Mr. Disc Jockey (1956)
Six Teens	A Casual Look (1956)
Kodaks	Teenager's Dream (1957)
Kodaks	Little Boy And Girl (1957)
Kodaks	Oh Gee Oh Gosh (1957)
Tune Weavers	Happy Happy Birthday Baby (1957)

Ten Best Doo-Wop Songs: All-Girl Groups, 1954-1957

Only ten all-girl group songs were chosen because of a dearth of songs to select from. Records featuring male groups backed by a female lead of the quality of Lillian Leach (Mellows), Pearl McKinnon (Kodaks), Yvonne Baker Mills (Sensations) and Ruth McFadden (Supremes) overshadowed the output of female-only groups during the early years of the doo-wop era.

Bonnie Sisters	Cry Baby	1956
Cookies	In Paradise	1956
Deltairs	Lullabye Of The Bells	1957
Hearts	Lonely Nights	1955
Hearts	He Drives Me Crazy	1956

Joytones	My Foolish Heart	1957
Peaches, Etta James & the	The Wallflower	1955
Queens, Shirley Gunter & the	Oop-Shoop	1954
Rosebuds	Dearest Darling	1957
Shepherd Sisters	Alone	1957

The Best Twenty Doo-Wop Songs By All-Girl Groups, 1958-1964

Starting in 1958, all-girl groups became more visible and started to hit the charts with regularity. The onslaught began with the Bobbettes, Chantels, Chordettes and Shirelles, and continued with the Crystals, Angels, Chiffons and Dixie Cups. Excluding coed groups led by females, our Top Twenty, 1958-1964, follow:

Angels	Til	1961
Angels	My Boyfriend's Back	1963
Aquatones	You	1958
Bobbettes	Mr. Lee	1957
Chantels	Maybe	1958
Chantels	Look In My Eyes	1961
Chiffons	He's So Fine	1963
Chiffons	One Fine Day	1963
Chordettes	Lollipop	1958

Clark, Claudine & the Spinners	Let Me In	1962
Cookies	Don't Say Nothin' (Bad About My Baby)	1963
Crystals	Da Doo Ron Ron	1963
Dixie Cups	Chapel Of Love	1964
Exciters	Tell Him	1962
Jelly Beans	I Wanna Love Him So Bad	1964
LaBelle, Patti & the Bluebelles	Down The Aisle (Wedding Song)	1963
Patti & the Emblems	Mixed-up, Shook-up Girl	1964
Poni-Tails	Born Too Late	1958
Shirelles	Tonight's The Night	1960
Shirelles	Mama Said	1961

The Girl Group Sound took over the charts from 1962-1964. Fifteen percent (4 of 26) of the group doo-wop records that charted on the R&B charts in 1961 were by all-girl groups or female-led groups. This increased to 22% in 1962 (11 of 49), then to 55% in 1963 (11 of 20) and 57% in 1964 (16 of 28). After 1964 the percent dropped off drastically because females started singing in different styles (e.g. the Supremes and the Shangri-Las). So the lady doo-woppers had their day in the sun, as the gentlemen doo-woppers had had before them. And then exited the stage.

What Were the Subjects of Doo-Wop?

The short answer is some combinations of birds, animals, flowers, gems, cars and more cars. And that's just the start. The doo-wop era had a slew of idiosyncratic processes involving the choice of group name, the choice of songs to record and even the subject matter and titles of the songs sung.

For some reason, doo-wop groups wanted us to know how many singers were in their group. In the "Complete Book of Doo-Wop," there were 136 "Fives" listed (e.g. Five Discs, Five Satins), 145 "Fours" and 30 "Threes." And 275 groups used the suffix or word "-tones" or "Tones" in their names. There are 18 groups called the "Dreamers" and 15 "Continentals." This last quirk is explainable that different groups could start singing, name themselves, not knowing that another quartet a few miles away had the same idea.

Group Names

The use of bird names started well before the doo-wop era, as in the Blackbirds of Harmony and Dixie Hummingbirds,[12] but certainly did take flight in it. The heightened affinity for bird doo-woppings no doubt started with the Ravens in 1946. Birds sing, ravens are black, so what better name for a singing group containing all black members? The Orioles followed, linking their name to the state bird of Maryland, as did Baltimore's baseball team when they moved from St. Louis. After the success of these two groups, others jumped on the bandwagon. What

---

[12] See, Moonoogian, G. A. Record Collector Monthly, Issue #51, July-Aug. 1992, p. 23.

follows is a list of 43 (omitting duplicates, meaning counting three Larks groups and one Larktones as one name, "Larks"), with the years in which they first recorded:

Ravens	1946
Orioles	1948
Bluebirds (The Four)	1949
Robins	1949
Cardinals	1951
Larks	1951
Skylarks	1951
Swallows	1951
Blue Jays	1953
Crows	1953
Flamingos	1953
Parrots	1953
Sparrows	1953
Swans	1953
Whipoorwills	1953
Buzzards (Big John & the)	1954
Eagles	1954
Feathers	1954
Hawks	1954
Parakeets	1954
Peacocks	1954
Pelicans	1954
Penguins	1954
Quails	1954
Starlings	1954
Wrens	1954

Birdies (Robert Byrd & His)	1956
Jay Birds	1956
Jayhawks	1956
Night Owls	1956
Drakes	1957
Ospreys	1957
Bobolinks	1958
Nighthawks	1958
Jays	1959
Doves	1960
Birds	1961
Nightingales	1961
Chicks (Kell Osborne & the)	1962
Hummingbirds	1962
Pheasants	1963
Ladybirds	1964
Whooping Cranes	1966

Running out of bird names, the singers moved on to naming themselves after various flavors of animals. Lots of felines, including Bengals (Bobby & the), Five Cats, Jaguars, Leopards, Lions, Panthers (Charles Watson & the), Tabbys, Tigers and Wildcats. There were invertebrates such as the Cobras, King Cobras, Sharks, Stingrays and Reptiles. Insects also, including flying, non-biting types (Butterflys, Lady Bugs), flying biters (Bees, Honey Bees, Fleas, Hornets and Mosquitoes) and crawlers/hoppers (Crickets, Grasshoppers, Roaches, Spiders and Termites). Miscellaneous mammals included the Bears, Cubs, Honey Bears, Chippendales, Colts, Mustangs, Anteaters, Beavers, Dolphins Ermines, Fawns, Gazelles, Impalas and Jackals, among others.

Other groups preferred flora to fauna, flowers being of particular interest. Eighteen groups are listed below, with the year they first recorded:

Carnations	1952
Blue Belles	1953
Orchids	1953
Daffodils	1955
Laurels	1955
Marigolds	1955
Blossoms	1957
Dahlias	1957
Gladiolas	1957
Hollyhocks	1957
Rosebuds	1957
Roses	1958
Goldenrods	1959
Tigre Lillies (sic)	1959
Lavenders	1960
Azaleas	1963
Bouquets	1963
Daisies	1964

Still other groups named themselves after precious stones and gems. Seventeen gem-type monikers were used, but because of duplication ((i.e. Rubies (1) and Rubies (2))) more than 60 groups fall under these names. They appear below with the year in which they first recorded:

Diamonds	1952
Crystals	1953

Jewels	1953
Rubies	1953
Blue Diamonds	1954
Emeralds	1954
Gems	1954
Opals	1954
Ivories	1956
Pearls	1956
Garnets	1957
Zircons	1957
Jades	1958
Sapphires	1958
Blue Crystals	1959
Ivorys	1962

Naming a group after a car or car model almost became an obsession with young singers. In 1954, the Cadillacs began recording and other groups followed in their dust. Esther Navarro, manager of the Cadillacs, said that the name was chosen because all the good bird names were already taken and a member of the group suggested "Cadillacs" after one passed by the window. Cadillacs' member Charlie Brooks had another version, stating that they named the group as they did to impress the ladies. There have been worse reasons.

Cars were always an expression and reflection of the male ego, so the idea to name your group after a car that you had or wanted was pretty compelling. As the first important car group, the Cadillacs took the most prestigious name available at the time. Lincolns and Chrysler Imperials were not as popular, the Packard was in decline, and the foreign showboats such as Jaguars, Mercedes and BMWs had not yet made significant inroads to the American market.

This was an age when American-made products were considered the best and anything "made in Japan" was met with derision. The range of car brands and models was much wider in the 1950s than it is today and many of the brands and models listed below aren't made any more. Also, General Motors outsold both Ford and Chrysler products, and choice of group names parallels this popularity. Below find group names, sorted by car company, brand within companies and model of car.

General Motors:

Chevrolet:	Belairs/Chevelles/Chevies/Corvairs/ Corvettes/El Caminos/Impalas/ Stingrays
Pontiac:	Bonnevilles/Catalinas/Tempests
Oldsmobile:	Deltas/Holidays/Starfires
Buick:	Centurys/Electras/Invictas/Rivieras/ Skylarks/Specials/Wildcats
Cadillacs	Caddys/Cadillacs/De Villes/ El Dorados/Fleetwoods

Chrysler:

Plymouth:	Belvederes/Furys/Satellites/Savoys Valiants
Dodge:	Coronets/Rams/Royals
Chrysler:	Chryslers/Imperials/New Yorkers/ Newports/Windsors

Ford:

  Ford: Fairlanes/Falcons/Galaxies/Mustangs/
                Thunderbirds/T-Birds
  Mercury: Mercurys/Meteors/Monarchs/
                Montereys
  Lincoln: Continentals/Lincolns
  Edsel: Edsels

American Motors:

  Nash: Metropolitans
  Rambler: Ambassadors/Ramblers/Rebels/
                Matadors

Misc. American:

  Studebaker: Avantis/Hawks/Studebaker "7"
  Packard: Packards
  Checker: Checkers
  Jeep: Cherokees
  Shelby: Cobras

Foreign:

  British: Bentleys/Healeys/Jaguars/Phaetons/
                Rovers/Sunbeams/Triumphs
  French: Renaults
  German: Merceedees (misspelled)
  Italian: Fiats/Spiders

Here are a few other trends in group naming:

Baseball teams:	Angels/Astros/Blue Jays/ Cardinals/Cubs/Dodgers/ Mariners/Orioles/(Swinging) Phillies/Pirates/Royals/Tigers/ (Hong Kong) White Sox
Board/Card games	Checkers/Dominoes/Chessmen/ Kings/Queens/Bishops/Knights/ Pawns/Castle Kings/Checkmates
World Citizens:	
Asia:	Orientals/Orients/Saigons
North America:	Canadian Meteors (Buddy Burke & the)/U.S. Four
Middle East:	Arabian Knights (Haji Baba & the)/Arabians/Egyptians/ Moroccans/Moroccos/Persians/ Persianettes/Tunisians (Terry & the)
Europe:	Belgianettes/Bohemians/Danes/ Francettes/Gypsies/Parisians/ Romans/Scotties/Venetians (Nick Marco & the)
Caribbean:	Bermudas/Caribbeans/ Carribeans/Cubans/Martineques /Trinidads
South America:	Ecuadors/Equadors

It seems that doo-wop singers looked to their own lives and environments to find a name for their group. This contrasts with other eras where the names are less concrete. Witness: Strawberry Alarm Clock, Cream, Rascals, Backstreet Boys, Nirvana, Abba and One Direction. Incidentally, an expanded list of these categories of doo-wop group names can be found in "The Complete Book of Doo-Wop," cited earlier.

Doo-Wop Songs Recorded Most Often

Over The Rainbow

The three songs recorded most often during the doo-wop era had their roots in earlier eras. The song most recorded, "Over The Rainbow," was written in 1939 by Harold Arlen and E.Y. Harburg. It was first recorded by Judy Garland for the Movie "The Wizard of Oz," which won the Oscar for best song of that year. In doo-wop, the title was at times lengthened to "Somewhere Over The Rainbow," and the lyrics simplified to fit the doo-wop style, and was usually rendered as a ballad. The most well-known doo-wop versions are by David Campanella (son of Roy Campanella, M.V.P. catcher for the erstwhile Brooklyn Dodgers) & the Delchords in 1959 and the Demensions in 1960. The latter spent nine weeks on the Billboard Charts, reaching number 16. Forty versions are listed below:

Castelles	1954
Checkers	1954
Dominoes	1955
Moroccos ("Somewhere...")	1956
Del Vikings ("Somewhere...")	1957
Echoes	1957
Mondellos (Yul McClay & the)	1957
Satisfiers	1957
Chanters (Bud Johnson & the)	1958
Hi-Liters	1958
Buddies (Little Butchie Saunders & the)	1959
Delchords (David Campanella & the) ("Somewhere...")	1959

Emjays	1959
Imperials (Little Anthony & the)	1959
Baysiders	1960
Demensions	1960
Delrons	1961
Guys (Little Sammy Rozzi & the)	1962
Monarchs	1962
Original Checkers	1962
Tones (Little Sammy & the)	1962
Vibrations	1962
Kac-Ties	1963
Darchaes (Nicky Addeo & the)	1964
Lytations (a cappella)	1964
Ricquettes (Danny Skeene & the)	1964
Young Ones (a cappella)	1964
Aztecs (Billy Thorpe & the)	1965
Blue Belles (Patti LaBelle & the)	1965
Five Fashions	1965
Mustangs	1965
Hamiltons (Alexander & the)	1966
Portraits	1968
Admirations	1972
Dell Vikings	1973
Marcels	1975
Image	1982
Deja-Vu	1984
Mystics	1987
Five Boroughs	1991

A Sunday Kind Of Love

   The tune recorded second-most was "A Sunday Kind Of Love," written by Barbara Belle, Louis Prima, Anita Leonard and Stan Rhodes in 1946. It was first recorded by Jo Stafford for Columbia records in 1947. It hit the doo-wop scene with the great standard version by the Harptones in 1953. In 1957 the Del Vikings put out an up-tempo arrangement that caught on and made the song a must-sing for groups of the era, though no version ever made the Billboard Top 40. Renditions are roughly divided between slow and fast versions and are often done a cappella. Twenty-nine are listed below:

Harptones	1953
Kings (Bobby Hall & the)	1953
Del Vikings	1957
Highlanders	1957
Sentimentals	1957
Lambert, Rudy (with the Lyrics)	1958
Gothics	1959
Winters, David (& group)	1959
Hollywood Saxons	1950s
High Seas	1960
Heard, Lonnie (with the Halos)	1961
Marcels	1961
Mystics	1961
Regents	1961
Persians	1962
Rapid-Tones (Willie Winfield & the)	1962
Roommates	1962

Camelots	1963
El Sierros	1963
Timetones	1963
Devotions	1964
Excellons	1964
Five Shadows	1965
Bees (Honey & the)	1968
Emery's	1977
Blue Moons	1960s
Earls	1975
Statics (Lynn & the)	1961
Five Boroughs	1988

Gloria

The third song to be discussed is "Gloria" which, by any measure, has the most interesting story behind it. Around 1946, Leon Rene of Exclusive Records, penned the original version. Three versions of this were recorded between 1946 and 1948, including one by the renowned Mills Brothers.

In 1954 however, another version appeared, written by Esther Navarro, the manager of the Cadillacs. This song was quite similar to Rene's version in that 1) the plot of unreturned love is in both, and 2) three lines, namely "Gloria, it's not Marie," "It's not Cherie" and "She's not in love with me (you)." The melodies, though similar, are not exact, Rene's being more sophisticated and less repetitive. We'll never know if the "borrowing" was intentional or not, but the two songs are clearly related.

The Cadillacs version soon became a streetcorner standard which, along with "Sunday Kind Of Love" became fodder for singers to strut their pipes on the street. Further, the name attracted songwriters like flies. In addition to groups that sang the Navarro version (e.g. Passions, Earl Lewis & the Channels, Vito & the Salutations), entirely new songs, with "Gloria" in the title, were issued. The Five Thrills, the Five Chances, the Chariots, Arthur Lee Maye & the Crowns and Hi-Lites put out different songs named "Gloria." The Frankie Grier Quartet put out "Oh Gloria," the Windsors "My Gloria" and the New Yorkers 5 "Gloria My Darling." Funny, since aside from "eu-" and "dysphoria," "trattoria" and "I wanna see more a ya," the word is pretty hard to rhyme with. Go figure. There's also a song called "Lover Boy" by the Gailtones which has the same melody as Navarro's Gloria, but substitutes "Lover Boy" in the lyrics. A list appears below:

Johnny Moore's Three Blazers (Rene version)	1946
Four Gabriels (Rene version)	1948
Mills Brothers (Rene version)	1948
Cadillacs (Navarro version)	1954
Five Thrills	1954
New Yorkers 5 ("... My Darling")	1955
Clefftones	1955
Crowns (Arthur Lee Maye & the)	1956
Five Chances	1956
Wallace, Jerry (& group)	1956
Clark, Dee (with the Kool Gents)	1957
Grier Quartet (The Frankie)	1958
Windsors (Lee Scott & the) ("My...")	1958

Chariots	1959
Passions	1960
Chapelaires	1961
Blue Knights (Steve Colt & the)	1962
Escorts	1962
Hi-Lites	1962
Parrish, Troy (with the Metallics)	1962
Salutations (Vito & the)	1962
Youngones (a cappella)	1962
Darchaes (Nicky Addeo & the)	1963
Del-Lourds	1963
Gems	1963
Vandells (Johnny Greco & the)	1963
Five Sharks (a cappella)	1964
Intruders	1964
Love Notes (Navarro version!)	1964
Ubans	
1964	
Savoys (a cappella)	1965
Sultans	1965
Dimucci, Dion (& group)	1969
Channels (Earl Lewis & the)	1971
Lanterns (a cappella)	1973
Newports	1981
Rubber Biscuits	1986

Doo-Wop Songs from After the Era

This section will pay homage to songs that (a) were recorded during the doo-wop era but not released until afterwards, and (b) songs recorded after the doo-wop era.

Late Releases

Vinyl record albums generally contained twelve tracks. When CDs came around they allowed for many more tracks, often as many as 25, if the tracks weren't too long. This allowed record companies to release songs that were sitting "in the can" for years, and to add out-takes. Twenty worthy songs, recorded during the era, but not released until later, appear below.

Group	Song	Year Rec.	Year Rel.
5 Bell-Aires	House Of Love	1960	1990
Bees	Sunny Side Of The Street	1955	1987
Cadillacs	Party For Two	1954	1983
Channels	Gloria	1956	1971
Chantels	So Real	1957	1987
Clefftones	Little Girl (I Love You Madly)	1955	1985
Clefftones	Gloria	1955	1985
Drifters	Three Thirty-Three	1954	1971
Fiestas	Things We Can't Forget	1959	1993
Flamingos	If I Could Love You	1956	1976

Hummers	Gee What A Girl	1956	1993
Imaginations	Mystery Of You	1962	1985
Jacks	Away	1955	1984
Kool Gents	Just Like A Fool	1956	1990s
Larks	All I Want For Christmas	1951	1988
Ravens	It's The Talk Of The Town	1950	1972
Solitaires	Come Back And Give Me Your Hand	1956	1984
Spiders	Love's All I'm Puttin' Down	1954	1992
Swallows	In The Palm Of My Hand	1958	1992
Vocal Teens	Be A Slave	1960	1972

Songs from After the Doo-Wop Era

Compact discs also allowed the proliferation of new material. What seems to work best and be appreciated most is when the composers and artists try to reproduce the sound and feel of original material sung during the actual doo-wop era. Twenty tracks that have accomplished this are listed below:

Blue Emotions	Doo-Wop All Night Long	1982
Bon-Aires	Cherry	1976
Capris	Morse Code Of Love	1982

Arthur Lee Maye/group	Moonlight	1985
Arthur Lee Maye/group	I'm Happy And In Love	1985
Cleftones	My Angel Lover	1990
Crystalaires	Teenage Ding Dong Bells	1990
Dahills	She's An Angel	1978
Dell Vikings	My Heart	1991
Dubs	Where To We Go From Here	1973
Earls	Dreams Come True	1973
Earls	All Through Our Teens	1976
Exodus	M & M	1971
Fabulous Dudes	Betty Blue Moon	1994
Joel, Billy & group	For The Longest Time	1984
Jaynells	One In A Million Girls	1984
Rob-Roys, N. Fox &	Lover Doll	1990
Globetrotters	Rainy Day Bells	1974
Storytellers	Please Remember My Love	1990
Tuneweavers (Margo Sylvia &)	Come Back ToMe	1989

Geographical Styles of Doo-Wop

Today, everyone can be connected to everyone else, not only in their own city or state, but around the world, just about instantaneously. "Psy" (Park Jae-sang), a South Korean singer/dancer became known world-wide for his hit single "Gangnam Style" within weeks. And who can forget the Macarena craze? Going "viral," meaning spreading wide and fast, is now in our lexicon.

In the fifties, that's not the way things worked. In order for influence to spread in music, the influencers had to be heard. This could happen in one of two ways. The influencees could either grow up in the same neighborhood or city as an influential group and hear their output directly, or they could hear them as a result of making a record, through radio play or purchase. Back then, not everyone could record. Cutting records was an investment so that only the really good artists got to make them. (Think of the difference in cost of taking a snapshot on film versus digital photography, which is basically free.)

A recording date for a particular record only carved in stone how much influence a group had incorporated into their music. A release date only indicated the date after which a group could, emphasis on could, influence others. No influence occurred unless the record received good airplay.

The importance of local neighborhood influence cannot be overstated. When Frankie Lymon & the Teenagers hit it big in 1956, there were a whole bunch of groups that followed with the schoolboy style. And all from the same area of the country, namely within a few miles of Sugar Hill (upper Manhattan in New York City). Among others, they were Lewis Lymon & the Teenchords, Schoolboys, Desires, Elchords, Valchords and Bobby Rivera & the Hemlocks. The success of the Teenagers brought label owners out of the woodwork and the place they looked for talent was in the Teenagers' back yard.

Since the technology of the era was quite primitive compared to what exists today, musical styles traveled much more slowly. Kids heard local groups over the radio everywhere, but west coast records only made it to New York airwaves (and vice versa) if they made the national charts, which few doo-wop songs did, at least in the mid-fifties. The Penguins "Earth Angel," on Dootone, a west coast label, was picked up and covered by the Crew Cuts on Mercury, a major label with wide distribution.

Most deejays and record companies were geographically nepotistic, giving an edge to local groups and sounds, hoping to strike gold without spending too much to search for talent. So teens generally heard slightly different doo-wop music, depending upon where they grew up. Philly teens heard more shrill tenors, Chicago kids heard more mournful ballads and bluesier jumps, Los Angelenos grew up on looser harmonies and New Yorkers heard more schoolboy and gang sounds. In 1954, a Philly teen heard the Castelles, Capris and Belltones, groups not well-known outside that city. The Orchids, Five Chances and Delighters met success in Chicago, but were unknown to New Yorkers. And the Fascinators, Ladders and Legends were legends in New York, but not elsewhere.

An extreme example of this hometown effect was reported to us by Peter Brown in 1997,[13] who at that time was writing for the Copley News Service. He grew up in Texas and New Mexico, and his exposure to rhythm and blues was via the cover records of Gail Storm, Pat Boone and the Crew Cuts. He had never heard black versions of his favorite songs, despite listening to a lot of local radio and trolling record stores. When he heard the real thing he was floored.

---

[13] Phone conversation, Feb. 19, 1997. First reported in "The Complete Book of Doo-Wop."

The result is that we must understand that one man's meat is another man's poison. We consider our Top 1000 as the best because we're writing the book. That's partially why there's room for notes on each page so the reader can write down their own preferences or scribble profanities aimed at the taste of these authors.

Seriously though, in "The Complete Book of Doo-Wop" we solicited help from people knowledgable in doo-wop from different areas of the country. First, we sought experts in the four major fonts of doo-wop: New York, Chicago, Los Angeles and Philadelphia. Their task was to tell us abut the rhythm & blues and/or doo-wop music created in their fair cities, to help us distinguish it from music created elsewhere and to give us a set of fifty representative songs. We then added two more opinions. One from the Baltimore-D.C. area because the Capitol area was important in providing influential groups such as the Orioles, Cardinals, Swallows and Four Buddies in the early 1950s. The second is a description of the "Southern Sound," and amalgamation of musics that came from a variety of places such as Nashville, New Orleans, Texas and the Virginia shore. Each writer had a different way of approaching their assignment, as will be clear in the pages that follow.

We've also calculated a measure of "concordance," which is the percent of songs on each list of 50 that appear on our Top 1000. These authors were born and raised in New York so it will come as no surprise that concordance is highest between Ronnie I's Top 50 and our Top 1000. Testimony from the six experts appears below along with their Top 50s. Quotes are taken from "The Complete Book of Doo-Wop."

Baltimore/D. C. by Nay Nasser

"While residing five years in Baltimore, I hosted a radio show which I named 'Echoes of the Past.' This weekly three-hour excursion into the roots of group harmony provided the opportunity to not only share my music, but to learn how the Baltimore-Washington D.C. region differed in group harmony.

...This fertile metropolitan area produced some of the finest vocal groups and sounds that this country has put to wax. The group records from 1951-1956 emanating from this region are generally characterized by a bluesy, melancholy mood on the ballads, while the uptempo sides do not generally have the sax break that shows up regularly on the New York sound. Early efforts by the Orioles, Clovers and Swallows seem to fit these generalizations. Once you get to 1957 and later, the Baltimore/Washington groups tend to sound much like their New York counterparts, at least stylistically.

I will attempt to list my favorite 50 vocal group records by groups from this region. My favorite group sounds come primarily from the 1957-1963 era. If you expect to see a lot of national hits or well-known group records, you've come to the wrong place."

Authors' notes: Nasser breaks his Top 50 into two equal parts; local Baltimore/D.C. artists on non-local labels (because many groups traveled to the big cities to record) and local/regional groups on local/regional labels. His comment that one shouldn't expect many national hits on his list bears out. Concordance is only 12%, that is only six of his 50 records are on our Top 1000, and all of the six are on non-local labels. That should not be taken to mean that this geographical area was ignored on the Top 1000. The six concordant groups (Cardinals, Clovers, Orioles, Rainbows, Ramblers and Swallows) account for 35 songs on our list and adding his other groups yields 41 songs.

Nasser just chose not to overemphasize these groups in his list.

Also, Nay Nasser was the only one of the six guests who added flip sides (which are included). His list has a wide range of years, from 1952 to 1968.

Baltimore/D. C. Artists on Non-Local Labels

1) Swallows	Beside You/You Left Me	1952	King 4225
2) Orioles	Crying In The Chapel/Don't You Think I Ought To Know	1953	Jubilee 5122
3) Four Buddies	My Mother's Eyes/Ooh-Ow	1953	Savoy 888
4) Magic-Tones	When I Kneel Down To Pray/Good Home "Googa Mooga"	1953	King 4665
5) Ramblers	Vadunt-Un-Va-Da Song/Please Bring Yourself Back	1954	MGM 11850
6) Cardinals	The Door Is Still Open/Misirlou	1955	Atlantic 1054
7) Rainbows	Mary Lee/Evenng	1955	Red Robin 134
8) Clovers	Devil Or Angel/Hey Doll Baby	1956	Atlantic 1083
9) Sonnets	Why Should We Break Up/Please Won't You	1956	Herald 477
10) Plants	Dear I Swear/It's You	1957	J&S 1602
11) Bachelors	After/You Know You Know	1957	Poplar 101
12) Sam Hawkins	King Of Fools/The Watchamacallit	1958	Gone 5042
13) Starlighters	I Cried/You're The One To Blame	1959	End 1049
14) Cruisers	Crying Over You/Don't Tease Me	1960	V-Tone 214
15) Twylights	Darling Let's Fall In Love/I'm Gonna Try	1961	Rock'n 102
16) Van McCoy	That's How Much You Mean To Me/I Wantcha	1961	Rock'n 100
17) George Jackson & the Unisons	Watching The Rainbow/Miss Frankenstein	1962	Lescay 3006
18) Trueleers	Waiting For You/Forget About Him	1962	Checker 1026
19) Van Dykes	Stupidity/King Of Fools	1962	Atlantic 2161
20) Billy Stewart	Wedding Bells//True Fine Lovin'	1962	Chess 1835
21) Connie Christmas	What A Night What A Morning/Big Chief	1962	Checker 1015
22) Freddy Owens	Bye Bye Baby/What Kind Of Heart	1962	Bethehem 3036
23) Paramounts	Shedding Teardrops/In A Dream	1963	Ember 1099
24) Belairs	Where Are You/Tell My Why	1963	X-Tra 113
25) Brenda & the Tabulations	Dry Your Eyes/The Wash	1967	Dionn 500

26)	Twilighters	Please Tell Me You're Mine/Wondering	1953	Marshall 702
27)	Kings	Angel/Come On Little Baby	1958	Jalo 203
28)	Little "D" & the Delighters	Oh My Darling/A Love So Fine	1958	Little "D" 1010
29)	Coolbreezers	The Greatest Love Of All/Ed Weda Bug	1958	Bale 101
30)	Truetones	Honey Honey/Whirlwind	1958	Monument 4501
31)	Kings	Surrender/Hold Me	1959	Jay Wing 5805
32)	Napoleon Tyce	Sitting Here/Paper Doll	1960	Norwood 105
33)	Gales	I Love You/Squeeze Me	1960	Winn 916
34)	Kenny Hamber	Tears In My Eyes/Do The Hully Gully	1960	Spar 101
35)	Kings	I Want To Know/Bump-I-Dy Bump	1960	Lookie 18
36)	Marvells	For Sentimental Reasons/Come Back	1961	Winn 1916
37)	Goldentones	I'm So Lonely/If I Had The Wings Of An Angel	1961	YRS 1001
38)	The Kid	Sleep Tight/True Love	1961	Rumble 1347
39)	Curley Bridges & Motley Crew	A Prayer Of Love/Yeah Let's Fly	1961	DC 0436
40)	Senators	Wedding Bells/I Shouldn't Care	1962	Winn 1917
41)	Tippie & the Clovermen	Please Mr. Sun/Gimme Gimme Gimme	1962	Stenton 7001
42)	Goldentones	Without You/Journey Bells	1962	YRS 1002
43)	Satisfactions	We Will Walk Together/Oh Why	1962	Chesapeake 610
44)	Four Jewels	Johnny Jealousy/Someone Special	1963	Start 638
45)	Little Hooks & the Kings	Count Your Blessings/How To Start A Romance	1963	Century 1300
46)	Vic Marcel	Come Back To These Arms/That's My Girl	1963	Don But 17349
47)	Veltones	I Want To Know/My Dear	1964	Wedge 1013
48)	Larks	Love You So/Love Me True	1965	Jett 3001
49)	Ebbtides	Come On And Cry/Straightaway	1965	Monumental 520
50)	Bleu Lights	Forever/They Don't Know My Heart	1968	Bay Sound 67003

New York City by Ronnie Italiano

"The Apollo Theater became a showcase for R&B artists and groups by the early 1950s. It provided a major route for the R&B gospel to be spread. Its location was naturally ideal for Harlem youngsters, who frequented the Apollo, to see their heroes in such groups as the Orioles, Ravens, Five Keys, Dominoes, Cardinals, Four Buddies, Larks, Five Royales, etc.

Teenagers began to congregate on street corners, in hallways and alleys, to imitate those Apollo Theater celebrities, whose recordings were so accessible in local record stores. The easiest way for a youngster to gain prestige in his neighborhood, become popular with the girls, and possibly make a little money while having fun, was to be discovered by a representative of one of the local independent record companies. The rapidly growing marketability of vocal groups resulted in frequent contract-signing by many of these "streetcorner troubadours."

"...In the beginning, New York didn't have its own sound, instead being influenced by the R&B feel of the Orioles, the gospel wailings of the Dominoes and the pop sound of the Ravens. In the 1950s, New York developed its own sound, being more polished that the high-tenor sound of Philadelphia or the bluesy sound of Chicago. Lead singers were sweet tenors, and the songs had a lot more bass riffs and introductions. The New York sound 'keyed' or leaned on the bass, which was used not as a lead, but to keep the tempo. The falsetto lead was also more present in New York in the 1950s than anywhere else, as in the songs of the Paragons, Jesters, Charts, Ladders, Mello-Harps and Legends, before it was taken over by the California groups of the 1960s. And of course, the kiddie sound was a New York original."

Authors' Notes: One can tell these authors were born and raised in New York City. Concordance is 78%, meaning that 39 of Ronnie I's 50 songs are on our Top

1000. Further, of the 11 songs on his list that are not on ours, all but two of the groups that sang them (Love Letters and Sonics) are not on our list. We just chose different songs. In fact, Ronnie I's Top 50 contains songs by 42 different groups. The 40 groups that are also on our Top 1000 sang 134 of our 1000 top songs.

Also note that Ronnie I's list uses a much more restricted range of years than did Nay Nasser's, going from 1952 to 1959 only.

1)	Diamonds	A Beggar For Your Kisses	1952	Atlantic 981
2)	Harptones	I'll Never Tell	1953	Bruce 101
3)	Crickets	For You I Have Eyes	1953	MGM 11507
4)	Mello-Moods	Call On Me	1953	Prestige 799
5)	Vocaleers	Is It A Dream	1953	Red Robin 114
6)	Velvets	I	1953	Red Robin 122
7)	Rivileers	Eternal Love	1954	Baton 205
8)	Master-Tones	Tell Me	1954	Bruce 111
9)	Coins	Blue, Can't Get No Place With You	1954	Gee 10
10)	Mellows	How Sentimental Can I Be	1954	Jay Dee 793
11)	Teardrops	The Stars Are Out Tonight	1954	Josie 766
12)	Strangers	Blue Flowers	1954	King 4709
13)	Solitaires	Wonder Why	1954	Old Town 1000
14)	Solitaires	Please Remember My Heart	1954	Old Town 1006
15)	Crows	Miss You	1954	Rama 30
16)	Wrens	Beggin' For Love	1954	Rama 53
17)	Fi-Tones Quintette	It Wasn't A Lie	1955	Atlas 1051
18)	Five Crowns	God Bless You	1955	Gee 1011
19)	Concords	Candlelight	1955	Harlem 2328
20)	Nutmegs	Ship Of Love	1955	Herald 459
21)	Heartbeats	Crazy For You	1955	Hull 711
22)	Cadillacs	Window Lady	1955	Josie 778
23)	Twilighters	Little Did I Dream	1955	MGM 55011
24)	Harptones	Life Is But A Dream	1955	Paradise 101
25)	Harptones	My Success (It All Depends On You)	1955	Paradise 103
26)	Four Fellows	Loving You Darling	1956	Glory 250
27)	Bop-Chords	Castle In The Sky	1956	Holiday 2601
28)	Heartbeats	Your Way	1956	Holiday 716
29)	Heartbeats	A Thousand Miles Away	1956	Hull 720
30)	Solitaires	Nothing Like A Little Love	1956	Old Town 1032
31)	Velours	My Love Come Back	1956	Onyx 501
32)	Valentines	Woo Woo Train	1956	Rama 196
33)	Continentals	Dear Lord	1956	Whirlin' Disc 101
34)	Love Letters	Walking The Streets Alone	1957	Acme 714
35)	Sunbeams	Please Say You'll Be Mine	1957	Acme 109
36)	Dubs	Don't Ask Me To Be Lonely	1957	Gone 5002
37)	Avons	Baby	1957	Hull 722
38)	Legends	Legend Of Love	1957	Hull 727
39)	Gaytunes	I Love You	1957	Joyce 101
40	Crests	Sweetest One	1957	Joyce 103
41)	Hurricanes	Priceless	1957	King 5042
42)	Keytones	Seven Wonders Of The World	1957	Old Town 1041
43)	Velours	This Could Be The Night	1957	Onyx 515
44)	Heartbeats	Everybody's Somebody's Fool	1957	Rama 231
45)	Matadors	Vengeance	1957	Sue 700
46)	Paragons	Let's Start All Over Again	1957	Winley 220
47)	Jesters	Please Let Me Love You	1957	Winley 221
48)	Du Mauriers	All Night Long	1958	Fury 1011
49)	Channels	My Love Will Never Die	1959	Fury 1021
50)	Sonics	This Broken Heart	1959	Harvard 801

Chicago Doo-wop by Robert Pruter

"...upon hearing many a Chicago group, one hears... a touch of gospel, a touch of blues, and an earthier feeling overall, so that one senses what is being heard is not a rock 'n roll, but a proto-soul recording."

"...The Chicago groups - unlike many groups in the South, notably the Larks and the Five Royales - were not simply gospel groups who merely secularized their lyrics with rhythm and blues themes. Rather, they were streetcorner groups like those in New York, but because they came straight up the Mississippi from the deep South - the heart of the deep gospel and blues sounds - their take on doo-wop is a bit more flavored by blues and gospel influences."

In the early 1960s, "...while New York was looking backward by experiencing a doo-wop revival period with belated recordings by the Shells, Capris, and Edsels hitting the charts - a revival that within a few years sank into degeneracy with the a cappella craze - Chicago was looking forward by creating new sounds. ...While one still heard doo-wop nonsense syllables in these transitional groups, the records incorporated more instrumentation and the groups sang with more intense funkier vocal stylings that in later years would inform soul music."

Authors' Notes: Pruter's list had the second highest concordance level: 52% with 26 of his listings on the Top 1000 list. The fifty choices comprised only 23 groups however, owing to the concentration on groups that achieved nationwide fame, such as the Flamingos, Moonglows, Spaniels, Dells and El Dorados. These groups placed 58 songs on the Top 1000. The range of years for his songs was 1953-1962.

1)	Coronets	Nadine	1953	Chess 1549
2)	Flamingos	Golden Teardrops	1953	Chess 1145
3)	Spaniels	Baby It's You	1953	Vee Jay 101
4)	Moonglows	Sincerely	1954	Chess 1581
5)	Spaniels	Goodnight Sweetheart, Goodnight	1954	Vee Jay 107
6)	Danderliers	My Autumn Love	1955	States 147
7)	Dells	Dreams Of Contentment	1955	Vee Jay 166
8)	El Dorados	At My Front Door	1955	Vee Jay 147
9)	El Dorados	I Began To Realize	1955	Vee Jay 165
10)	Five Chances	All I Want	1955	Blue Lake 115
11)	Five Notes	Park Your Love	1955	Chess 1614
12)	Five Notes	Show Me The Way	1955	Chess 1614
13)	Flamingos	I'm Yours	1955	Parrot 812
14)	Orchids	Newly Wed	1955	Parrot 815
15)	Orchids	You're Everything To Me	1955	Parrot 815
16)	Orchids	You Said You Loved Me	1955	Parrot 819
17)	Orchids	You Have Two (I Have None)	1955	Vee Jay (rel. 1993)
18)	Spaniels	You Painted Pictures	1955	Vee Jay 154
19)	Moonglows	Most Of All	1955	Chess 1589
20)	Danderliers	May God Be With You	1956	States 152
21)	Dells	Oh What A Nite	1956	Vee Jay 204
22)	Flamingos	I'll Be Home	1956	Checker 830
23)	Flamingos	A Kiss From Your Lips	1956	Checker 837
24)	Kool Gents	I Can't Help Myself	1956	Vee Jay 207
25)	Magnificents	Up On The Mountain	1956	Vee Jay 183
26)	Moonglows	We Go Together	1956	Chess 1619
27)	Spaniels	You Gave Me Peace Of Mind	1956	Vee Jay 229
28)	Gems	Til The Day I Die	1957	Drexel 915
29)	Spaniels	Everyone's Laughing	1957	Vee Jay 246
30)	Spaniels	I Lost You	1957	Vee Jay 264
31)	Spaniels	Here Is Why I Love You	1958	Vee Jay 290
32)	Bel Aires	My Yearbook	1958	Decca 30631
33)	Magnificents	Don't Leave Me	1958	Vee Jay 281
34)	Dells	Dry Your Eyes	1959	Vee Jay 324
35)	Bo Diddley	I'm Sorry	1959	Checker 914
36)	Bo Diddley	You Know I Love You	1959	Checker (rel. 1990)
37)	Moonglows	Twelve Months Of The Year	1959	Chess 1725
38)	Sheppards	Island Of Love	1959	Apex 7750
39)	Faith Taylor & theSweet Teens	I Need Him To Love Me	1959	Bea & Baby 104
40)	Spaniels	I Know	1960	Vee Jay 350
41)	Sheppards	Tragic (1961 Apex version)	1961	Apex 7762
42)	Sheppards	Queen Of Hearts	1961	Constellation LP4
43)	Sheppards	Forgotten	1961	Constellation LP4
44)	Swinging Hearts	Please Say It Isn't So	1961	Lucky Four 1011
45)	Vibrations	Oh Cindy	1961	Checker 1002
46)	Dukays	Night Owl	1961	Nat 4002
47)	Gene Chandler (Dukays)	Duke Of Earl	1961	Vee Jay 416
48)	Daylighters	Whisper Of The Wind	1962	Tip Top 2007
49)	Uniques	Silvery Moon	1962	Lucky Four 1024
50)	Donald & the Delighters	(Native Girl) Elephant Walk	1962	Cortland 109

Los Angeles Group Records by Steve Propes

"The L.A. groups had a simplicity and feeling, an unpolished sincerity and earnestness. Many of these acts, especially the Central Avenue groups like the Lamplighters, early Platters, Turks, Penguins, Flairs and the various Jesse Belvin groups like the Clliques and Gassers, often practiced together and developed songs together. Gaynel Hodge of the early Platters and Turks would laughingly refer to this style as 'ice cream changes.' Whatever it was, it told a story that teens and record buyers of all ages, races and hometowns could identify with, love, and spend their few record-buying pennies on. When you listen to Vernon Green make up lyrics like 'pismotology' on 'The Letter' or Julian Herrera singing about remembering Linda, you somehow knew that the experience was real and the motivation was to communicate this feeling. New York had the more polished 'doo-wop' style, Chicago had a bluesier sound, but for true feeling and sincerity with a lyric, a vocal, a spoken bridge, it was for that ingredient that you came to Los Angeles."

"...This L.A. sound stayed around for a good 15 years, shut down only by the transformation brought by the British Invasion and, more powerfully, by the Watts Riots in August of 1965. After that event, the link between Central Avenue/Watts and the recording industry in Hollywood and other more affluent neighborhoods, if not broken, certainly frayed. It also charged the music with a touch of anger, a harder edge, and a need to give out a social or political message sans love making, drinking wine, or fast cars, subjects that marked the earlier era."

Authors' Notes: Concordance was third highest, at 30%, with 15 of the songs on Propes' list appearing on our Top 1000. Propes spread the citations around, listing 46 different groups for his 50 songs. These 46 groups placed 48 songs on the Top 1000. Steve mentions that groups were fluid; forming, reforming and changing names quite often and centered around talented individuals like Jesse Belvin, Richard Berry, Gaynel Hodge, Cornel Gunter, Billy Jones and Tony Allen. The groups that were concordant with our list produced 48 songs on our Top 1000. The range of years is large; from 1950-1964.

1) Robins with Little Esther	Double Crossin' Blues	1950	Savoy 731
2) Hollywood Flames	Young Girl	1950	Recorded In Hollywood 165
3) Three Dots & A Dash/Jesse Belvin	All That Wine Is Gone	1951	Imperial 5115
4) Platters	Give Thanks	1953	Federal 12153
5) Lamplighters	Be Bop Wino	1953	Federal 12152
6) Flairs	She Wants To Rock	1953	Flair 1012
7) Hollywood Flames	I Know	1953	Swing Time 345
8) Robins	Riot In Cell Block #9	1954	Spark 103
9) Penguins	Earth Angel	1954	Dootone 348
10) Medallions	The Letter	1954	Dootone 347
11) Jewels	Hearts Of Stone	1954	R&B 1301
12) Flairs	This Is The Night For Love	1954	Flair 1044
13) Shirley Gunter & the Queens	Oop Shoop	1954	Flair 1050
14) Donald Woods & the Vel Aires	Death Of An Angel	1954	Flip 306
15) Tony Allen & the Chimes	Nite Owl	1955	Specialty 560
16) Squires	Sindy	1955	Mambo 105
17) Turks	Emily	1955	Money 211
18) Sheiks	Sentimental Heart	1955	Federal 12237
19) Jaguars	The Way You Look Tonight	1956	Aardell 0011
20) Jayhawks	Counting My Teardrops	1956	Flash 105
21) Twilighters	Eternally	1956	Cholly 712
22) Dots	I Confess	1956	Caddy 101
23) Cadets	Stranded In The Jungle	1956	Modern 994
24) Velveteers	Tell Me You're Mine	1956	Spitfire 15
25) Native Boys	Oh Let Me Dream	1956	Combo 120
26) Cliques	Girl In My Dreams	1956	Modern 987
27) Premiers	My Darling	1956	Dig 113
28) Six Teens	A Casual Look	1956	Flip 315
29) Jesse Belvin	Beware	1956	Cash 1056
30) Richard Berry & Pharaohs	Take The Key	1956	Flip 318
31) Little Julian Herrera/Tigers	I Remember Linda	1957	Starla 6
32) Eugene Church	Open Up Your Heart	1957	Specialty 604
33) Valiants	This Is The Night	1957	Keen 34004
34) Sharps	Six Months Three Weeks Two Days & An Hour	1957	Tag 2200
35) Jerry Stone & the Four Dots	It's Heaven	1958	Freedom 44002

36) Shields	You Cheated	1958	Tender 513
37) Storytellers	You Played Me A Fool	1959	Stack 500
38) Jaguars	Thinking Of You	1959	Original Sound 06
39) Pentagons	To Be Loved	1960	Fleet Int'l 100
40) Gallahads	Lonely Guy	1960	Donna 1322
41) Elgins	Uncle Sam's Man	1961	Flip 353
42) Little Sammy	Can You Love Me	1961	Shade 1002
43) Blue Jays	Lover's Island	1961	Milestone 2008
44) Atlantics	Boo Hoo Hoo	1961	Linda 103
45) Charles McCull- ough & the Silks	My Girl	1961	Dooto 462
46) Utopians	Along My Lonely Way	1962	Imperial 5876
47) Intervals	Here's That Rainy Day	1962	Class 204
48) Metallics	Need Your Love	1962	Baronet 2
49) Rivingtons	Cherry	1963	Liberty 55610
50) MM & the Peanuts	Open Up Your Eyes	1964	Money 101

The Singers of Philadelphia by Robert Bosco

"...the Castelles emitted an ethereal sound which captured the hearts and minds of local teens. Though largely unappreciated by the rest of the hemisphere... they prepped the public for such similar-sounding outfits as the Dreamers, the Dreams, the Belltones... the Angels and the odd-sounding Capris, whose lead shrieking by Rene Hinton..."

"On balance, the so-called Philadelphia sound, the one with all the high-tenor high jinx, was a short-lived phenomenon. It lasted about two to three years, and by 1956, it was confined, basically, to six square blocks in West Philly, virtually forgotten elsewhere... ...by 1957, the groups had more or less homogenized themselves, and those distinctive high-pitched wailings were yesterday's news."

Authors' Notes: Concordance was quite high, at 72%, 36 of Bosco's songs being on our Top 1000. Thirty-eight groups are represented and they contributed 56 songs to our Top 1000. The list covers the period 1953-1965, with one out-lier from 1992.

1) Buccaneers'	The Stars Will Remember	1953	Rama 21
2) Castelles	My Girl Awaits Me	1953	Grand 101
3) Angels	Wedding Bells (Are Ringing In My	1954	Grand 115
4) Angels	A Lovely Way To Spend An	1954	Grand 121
5) Belltones	Estelle	1954	Grand 102
6) Capris	God Only Knows	1954	Gotham 7304
7) Castelles	Over A Cup Of Coffee	1954	Grand 109
8) Swans	My True Love	1953	Rainbow 233
9) Lee Andrews & the Hearts	White Cliffs Of Dover	1954	Rainbow 256
10) Hide-A-Ways	Can't Help Loving That Girl Of Mine	1955	Ronni 1000
11) Turbans	When You Dance	1955	Herald 458
12) Lee Andrews & the Hearts	Lonely Room	1956	Gotham 320
13) Sensations	Please Mr. Disc Jockey	1956	Atco 6067
14) Keystoners	Magic Kiss	1956	Epic 9187
15) Blue Notes	If You Love Me	1956	Josie 800/Port 70021
16) Marquees	The Rain	1956	Grand 141
17) Danny & the Juniors	At The Hop	1957	Singular 711/ABC 9871
18) Fabulaires	While Walking	1957	East West 103/Main Line 103
19) Lee Andrews &	Long Lonely Nights	1957	Grand 157/Main LIne 102
20) Silhouettes	Get A Job	1957	Junior 391/Junior 593
21) Superiors	Lost Love	1957	Atco 6106/Main Line 104
22) Turbans	Congratulations	1957	Herald 510
23) Universals	Again	1957	Mark-X 7004
24) Re-Vels	So In Love	1958	Teen 122
25) Lee Andrews & the Hearts	Try The Impossible	1958	Casino 452/UA 123
26) Re-Vels	False Alarm	1958	Chess 1708
27) Sharmeers	A School Girl In Love	1958	Red Top 109
28) Silhouettes	Bing Bong	1958	Ember 1037
29) Boss-Tones	Mope-Itty Mope	1959	Boss 401/V-Tone 208
30) Herb Johnson & the Premiers	Help	1959	Palm 301

31) Blue Notes	My Hero	1960	Val-Ue 213/Red Top 135
32) Herb Johnson &	Have You Heard	1960	Len 1007
33) Dreamlovers	When We Get Married	1961	Heritage 102
34) Dovells	Bristol Stomp	1961	Parkway 827
35) Lydells	Wizard Of Love	1961	Master 251
36) Sensations	Let Me In	1961	Argo 5405
37) Orlons	Mr. 21	1962	Cameo 211
38) Sundials	Chapel Of Love	1962	Guyden 2065
39) Billy & the Essentials	Maybe You'll Be There	1962	Jamie 1239
40) Little Joey & the Flips	Bongo Stomp	1962	Joy 262
41) Majors	A Wonderful Dream	1962	Imperial 5855
42) Anthony & the Sophomores	Play Those Oldies Mr. D.J.	1963	Mercury 72103
43) Whirlwinds	Heartbeat	1963	Phillips 40139
44) Contenders	The Clock	1963	Long Fiber 201
45) Intentions	Summertime Angel	1963	Jamie 1253
46) Rick & the Masters	Let It Please Be You	1963	Cameo 247
47) Tymes	So In Love	1963	Parkway 871A
48) Four J's	Here Am I Broken Hearted	1964	Jamie 1267
49) Billy & the Essentials	The Actor	1965	Cameo 344
50) Keystoners	Gossip	1992	Starbound 515

Southern R'n'B Vocal Groups by Gordon Skadberg

"The genre of R 'n' B vocal group music had its beginnings in large United States cities such as Baltimore, New York, Chicago and Los Angeles. However, it wasn't long before this young art form spread throughout the country, especially to its roots in the South. The result was quite different from the R 'n' B beginnings in Baltimore, the street corner feel of New York, the bluesy vocals of Chicago, and the dreamy mood of Los Angeles. Instead a unique sound of gospel-flavored harmonies, country lyrics, and somewhat raw vocal stylings was created; the southern sound of vocal group harmony."

Authors' Notes: Skadberg had, by far, the toughest assignment of the six contributors. Melding the sounds of bluesy New Orleans, country-style Nashville influences, the Texas twang, and beach music is a formidable task. Of all the southern locales, New Orleans was probably the most important, producing the Spiders, an almost-supergroup that had a few chart successes in the 1950s.

Concordance was low at 20%, 10 songs being on our Top 1000. Gordon listed 43 groups, but all told, they only placed 18 songs on our list of 1000 songs. He also provided us with a narrow band of years from which the songs were drawn: 1953-1960.

1) Bobby Mitchell & the Toppers	One Friday Morning	1953	Imperial 5250
2) Prisonaires	Just Walking In The Rain	1953	Sun 186
3) Prisonaires	My God Is Real	1953	Sun 189
4) Varieteers	If You And I Could Be Sweethearts	1953	Hickory 1014
5) Hawks	Candy Girl	1954	Imperial 5266
6) Pelicans	Chimes	1954	Imperial 5307
7) Bees	Toy Bell	1954	Imperial 5314
8) Tempo Toppers	Rice, Red Beans And Turnip Greens	1954	Peacock 1628
9) Clefs	I'll Be Waiting	1954	Peacock 1643
10) Hawketts	Mardi Gras Mambo	1955	Chess 1591
11) Marigolds	Rollin' Stone	1955	Excello 2057
12) Thunderbirds	Love Is A Problem	1955	GG 518
13) Kidds	Are You Forgetting Me	1955	Imperial 5335
14) Barons	Eternally Yours	1955	Imperial 5343
15) Jewels	Hearts Can Be Broken	1955	Imperial 5351
16) Spiders	Bells In My Heart	1955	Imperial 5354
17) Barons	My Dear, My Love	1955	Imperial 5359
18) Spiders	Witchcraft	1955	Imperial 5366
19) Scamps	Waterproof	1955	Peacock 1655
20) Sharptones	Made To Love	1955	Post 2009
21) Five Tones	Sitting By My Window	1955	Sun 222
22) Five Owls	Pleading To You	1955	Vulcan 1025
23) Kool Toppers	Cause I Love You	1955	Beverly 702
24) Evergreens	Very Truly Yours	1955	Chart 605
25) Dukes	Teardrop Eyes	1956	Imperial 5401
26) Dukes	Cotton Pickin' Hands	1956	Imperial 5415
27) Majestics	Nitey Nite	1956	Marlin 802
28) Esquires	Only The Angels Know	1956	Hi-Po 1003
29) Trutones	Magic	1957	Chart 634
30) Supremes	Just For You And I	1957	Ace 534
31) El Torros	Dance With Me	1957	Duke 175
32) Sultans	If I Could Tell	1957	Duke 178
33) Gladiolas	Little Darling	1957	Excello 2101
34) Gladiolas	Hey Little Girl	1957	Excello 2120
35) Five Chums	Give Me The Power	1957	Excello 2123
36) Hollyhocks	Don't Say Tomorrow	1957	Nasco 6001
37) Rockin Dukes	Angel And A Rose	1957	OJ 1007
38) Uniques	Somewhere	1957	Peacock 1677
39) Five Royales	Dedicated To The One I Love	1957	King 5098
40) Capistranos	Now Darling	1958	Duke 179
41) Sensational Dellos	Lost Love	1958	Mida 109
42) Chester McDow-ell & group	I Wonder Why	1959	Duke 302
43) King Crooners	Now That's She's Gone	1959	Excello 2168

44) King Crooners	Won't You Let Me Know	1959	Excello 2168
45) King Crooners	She's Mine All Mine	1959	Hart 1002
46) Berrycups	Hurt By A Letter	1959	Khoury's 710
47) Lyrics	Oh Please Love Me	1959	Wildcat 0028
48) Huey Smith & group	Dearest Darling	1959	Ace 571
49) El Torros	What's The Matter	1960	Duke 321
50) Royal Jesters	My Angel Of Love	1960	Harlem 105

Other Geographical Fonts of Doo-Wop

New York absorbed the sounds of its neighbors, Connecticut and New Jersey. Most of the Connecticut groups came out of New Haven, like the Nutmegs, Scarlets/Five Satins, Four Haven Knights, Chestnuts, Academics and Hi-Lites. All of these groups, with the exception of the Academics (who had a good white group sound) produced melodic ballads with heavy backbeats and many doo-wop characteristics. Probably because of cross-fertilization, the groups have as many things in common with New York groups as they have with each other, so it is hard to justify establishing a "Connecticut Sound."

Groups from New Jersey met a similar fate. The Avons, Kodaks, Monotones, Fiestas, Keytones, Ambassadors and Gentlemen all came from cities in Northern New Jersey, a stone's throw away from New York. Most also recorded for labels that were headquartered in New York (as did Connecticut groups), making it even tougher to distinguish a "New Jersey Sound" from a New York one.

Detroit was to Chicago as Connecticut and New Jersey were to New York. Detroit was a real player, spawning the Royals/Midnighters, Diablos, Pearls, Falcons and Don Juans. The sound of these groups was basically bluesy, which some have described as proto-soul, and Nolan Strong of the Diablos is thought to be the harbinger of the Motown sound, Great music, but very akin to what was coming out of Chicago at around the same time (the mid-1950s).

The Boston area had a bunch of groups, like the G-Clefs from Roxbury, the Love-Notes, the Jamies and, of course, the Tune Weavers. It's tough to get a handle on the Boston sound though, except that it is fairly rock 'n' rollish and not overly streetcornerish.

Finally, Pittsburgh had some big-name groups, such as the Dell Vikings, the Skyliners and Marcels, and a few minor ones, like the El Capris and Capitols. Aside from often having a big bass part, the songs are pretty hard to characterize.

As an epilogue, it is to be noted that the differences among the four major locations narrowed, by degrees, as the 1950s drew to a close. The passage of time allowed for cross-fertilization of one geographical style to another. Fewer and fewer groups adhered to the original sound of their city and some groups just stopped recording, so what emerged in the 1960s was a generic doo-wop style which probably fell closest to the New York style, or to other musics, such as Chicago soul or Philly rock 'n' roll.

In sum, the task assigned to the six guest authors was to "tell us about the rhythm and blues and/or doo-wop created in their fair cities, to help us to distinguish it from music created elsewhere, and to give us a set of representative songs."

Because of the nature of the assignment, one should not expect their lists to coincide highly with ours. We asked for "representative songs," not "best songs." And we asked for songs that helped us "distinguish" among styles, basically biasing their choices toward stereotypical local songs. This is particularly evident in the Top 50s from Baltimore and Philadelphia.

In all, 110 songs out of 300 on these six Top 50s coincide with songs on our Top 1000 list. That means that 190 (300 -110) of their songs are not on our list. That's okay, it gives the reader 190 more tracks to hunt down!

Still More Opinions

Aside from presenting geographical differences in the doo-wop sound, we offer four different opinions by people/audiences that were important in the historical arc taken by our music. The first is from the fabled Irving "Slim" Rose's Times Square Records, arguably the center of the doo-wop world, circa 1961.

Second we list the favorite songs of Gus Gossert, a charismatic dee-jay that inspired a second generation of doo-wopcentrists around 1970. Third is a list of 101 songs yielded by a WCBS-FM survey of fans of Don K. Reed's Doo-Wop Shop in the early 1990s. And last, the Top 100 arrived at in a U.G.H.A. survey of its members in the late 1990s.

Times Square Records Top 100 (sales), January, 1961

Slim Rose is credited with making the music popular again (although he had much help from a number of his young part-time employees) in the 1959-1964 time frame. His shop, in the Times Square subway station, was the hub of vocal group music and attracted white teens from all over the New York metropolitan area. Slim preferred the sound of "kiddie" leads a la Frankie Lymon, which also reflected the tastes of his young white customers. Below find one of Slim's lists:

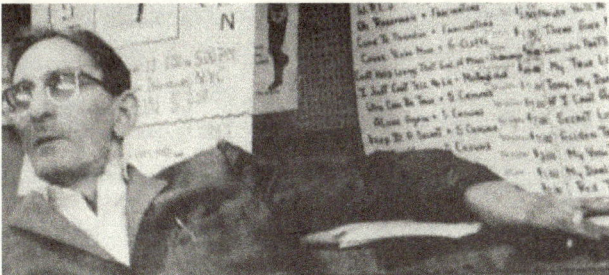

1	Five Discs	I Remember	1958
2	Edsels	Lama Rama Ding Dong	1958
3	Admirations	The Bells Of Rosa Rita	1959
4	Elchords	Peppermint Stick	1958
5	Capris	There's A Moon Out Tonight	1959
6	Hi-Fives	Dorothy	1958
7	Channels	I Really Love You	1957
8	Channels	Flames In My Heart	1957
9	Continentals	Picture Of Love	1957
10	Students	Every Day Of The Week	1958
11	Cineramas	Life Can Be Beautiful	1958
12	Roulettes	I See A Star	1958
13	Chanters	No, No, No	1957
14	Chanters	Row Your Boat	1957
15	Chanters	Five Little Kisses	1957
16	Chanters	My, My Darling	1957
17	Deltas	Lamplight	1957
18	Jive-Tones	Ding Ding Dong	1958
19	Dubs	Don't Ask My To Be Lonely	1958
20	Bluenotes	If You Love Me	1956
21	Desires	Let It Please Be You	1959
22	Selections	Guardian Angel	1959
23	Cadillacs	Gloria	1954
24	Delroys	Bermuda Shorts	1957
25	Cameos	Wait Up	1958
26	Vince Castro	Bong Bong	1958
27	Rocketones	Mexico	1957
28	Shells	Baby Oh Baby	1957
29	Jaguars	The Way You Look Tonight	1957
30	Van Dykes	The Bells Are Ringing	1957
31	Miracles	Bad Girl	1959
32	Channels	Bye, Bye Baby	1958
33	Schoolboys	Please Say You Want Me	1957
34	Rainbows	Mary Lee	1955
35	Crests	Sweetest One	1957
36	Velours	Can I Come Over Tonight	1957

37	Mellows	Smoke From Your Cigarette	1954
38	Deltairs	Lullaby Of The Bells	1958
39	Pyramids	Ankle Bracelet	1958
40	Bop-Chords	When I Woke Up This Morning	1957
41	Drifters	There Goes My Baby	1959
42	Monarchs	Pretty Little Girl	1956
43	Magnificents	Up On The Mountain	1956
44	Continentals	Dear Lord	1956
45	Emjays	This Is My Love	1958
46	Love-Notes	United	1957
47	Ladders	Counting The Stars	1957
48	Dubs	Chapel Of Dreams	1958
49	Charts	Desiree	1957
50	Kodaks	Teenagers Dream	1957
51	Channels	Gleam In Your Eye	1957
52	Isley Brothers	Shout	1959
53	Bonnevilles	Zu-Zu	1960
54	Solitaires	The Angels Sang	1956
55	Capris	God Only Knows	1954
56	Hemlocks	Cora Lee	1957
57	Shirelles	Dedicated To The One I Love	1959
58	Channels	The Closer You Are	1956
59	Rob-Roys	Tell My Why	1957
60	Dubs	Could This Be Magic	1957
61	Bluenotes	My Hero	1960
62	Heartbeats	People Are Talking	1956
63	Collegians	Let's Go For A Ride	1957
64	Chantels	I Love You So	1958
65	Clovers	Devil Or Angel	1956
66	Pastels	Been So Long	1957
67	Quinns	Hong Kong	1958
68	Little Anthony & the Imperials	Two People In The World	1958
69	Danleers	One Summer Night	1958

70	Eddie & the the Starlights	To Make A Long Story Short	1959
71	Heartbeats	Crazy For You	1955
72	Lincoln Fig & the Dates	Way Up	1958
73	Monotones	Book Of Love	1958
74	Heartbeats	A Thousand Miles Away	1956
75	Cleftones	Little Girl Of Mine	1956
76	Sentimentals	Sunday Kind Of Love	1958
77	Moonglows	We Go Together	1956
78	Channels	That's My Desire	1957
79	Lee Andrews & the Hearts	Bells Of St. Mary's	1954
80	Richard Lanham & the Tempo-Tones	On Your Radio	1956
81	Spaniels	Trees	1958
82	Adelphis	Kathleen	1958
83	Frankie Lymon & the Teenagers	Teenage Love	1957
84	Monotones	Legend Of Sleepy Hollow	1958
85	Diablos	The Wind	1954
86	Troys	Ding A Ling A Ling	1957
87	Duvals	You Came To Me	1955
88	Gladiolas	Little Darlin'	1957
89	Embers	Paradise Hill	1954
90	Valiants	This Is The Night	1958
91	Youngtones	You I Adore	1957
92	Cubs	Why Do You Make Me Cry	1957
93	Flamingos	Lovers Never Say Goodbye	1959
94	Videls	Be My Girl	1957
95	Mello-Harps	Gumma, Gumma	1958
96	Jeanie & Her Boyfriends	Baby	1959
97	Videos	Trickle, Trickle	1958
98	Nutmegs	Ship Of Love	1956
99	Nicky & the Nobles	School Bells	1957
100	Screamin' Jay Hawkins	I Put A Spell On You	1957

Gus Gossert's Top 40 All-Time Favorite Doo-Wopps

A second opinion is provided by Gus Gossert. Actually, not "the Gossert" himself, but from someone who knew his tastes quite well, Ronnie Italiano.[14] Gossert is credited with popularizing the term "doo-wop" when he moved to New York from the West Coast in 1959. Gossert

---

[14] Italiano, Ronnie. "Gus Gossert's Top 40 All-Time Favorite Doo-Wopps." *Time Barrier Express*, Issue #20, Nov.-Dec. 1976, p. 16.

got away with a lot of antics, such as eating pizza and burping on the air and sometimes being late for his own show. He was described as charismatic, cool and funny by those who knew him, but not an expert on the music. Just as Slim Rose had his young experts that guided him, so did Gossert. Eventually, his substance abuse led to both his being fired from his gig at WCBS-FM and his premature death at the age of 33 in Tennessee. He was found by a roadside. His list, via Ronnie I. follows:

1	Students	I'm So Young	1958
2	Ocapellos	The Stars	1966
3	Teenagers	Share	1956
4	Students	My Vow To You	1958
5	Fantastics	There Goes My Love	1959
6	Penguins	Memories Of El Monte	1963
7	Diablos	Since You've Been Gone	1958
8	King Pleasure	I'm In The Mood For Love	1959
9	Fascinators	Chapel Bells	1958
10	Charades	Please Be My Love Tonight	1963
11	Harptones	I'll Never Tell	1953
12	Five Keys	The Verdict	1955
13	Valentines	Don't Say Goodnight	1957
14	Shells	Deep In My Heart	1962
15	Harptones	A Sunday Kind Of Love	1953
16	Dubs	Be Sure My Love	1958
17	Fascinators	Who Do You Think You Are	1959
18	Admirations	The Bells Of Rosa Rita	1959
19	Bagdads	Bring Back Those Doo-Wopps	1963
20	Youngsters	You Told Another Lie	1958
21	Harptones	The Shrine Of St. Cecilia	1957
22	Nutmegs	Hello	1962
23	Youngtones	Can I Come Over	1960
24	Platters	I'm Just A Dancing Partner	1955
25	Pizza Pie	Rob Roys	1959
26	Students	Every Day Of The Week	1958
27	Harptones	My Memories Of You	1954

28	Charms	I'd Like To Thank You Mr. D.J.	1956
29	Crests	My Juanita	1957
30	Monotones	Soft Shadows	1958
31	Cleftones	String Around My Heart	1956
32	Nutmegs	Down In Mexico	1962
33	Dubs	Chapel Of Dreams	1958
34	Penguins	Love Will Make Your Mind Go Wild	1954
35	Five Keys	Close Your Eyes	1955
36	Diablos	The Wind	1954
37	Nobles	Poor Rock 'n' Roll	1957
38	Students	Mommy And Daddy	1958
39	Delacardos	Letter To A Schoolgirl	1959
40	Bluenotes	My Hero	1960

The WCBS-FM101 Top 101 Doo-Wop Songs of All Time (1993)

Listen to
Don K. Reed's
Doo-Wop Shop
Sundays 7PM-Midnight
On
WCBS-FM 101.1
New York's Oldies Station

WCBS-FM

TOP 101
DOO-WOP
SONGS OF
ALL TIME

101.1

The third list comes from a WCBS-FM (New York) poll of their listeners in the early 1990s. When Gossert was canned, he was replaced by Norm N. Nite, who initiated his "Nite Train Show" in 1972. In 1975 Norm left to return to his native Cincinatti after publishing the encyclopedic "Rock On," one of the first listings of current and past rock 'n' roll performers (including doo-wop groups). As of 2013 Norm is still active, broadcasting oldies on the Sirius network from the Rock 'n' Roll Hall of Fame in Cleveland.

The man who replaced him, Don K. Reed, renamed the show "The Doo-Wop Shop" and had an almost 30 year run with it. Don always played "meat and potatoes" doo-wops, the ones that most of his audience was familiar with and loved. His audience were not "purists," like the ones who belong to U.G.H.A. (see the next list). Their purpose is enjoyment rather than learning, the songs were whiter than those of the "purists" and were recorded later in the era. These songs are the heart and soul, the core, of the doo-wop era. A poll taken of Doo-Wop Shop listeners in the early 1990s follows:

1	Five Satins	In The Still Of The Night	1956
2	Penguins	Earth Angel	1954
3	Classics	Till Then	1963
4	Capris	Morse Code Of Love	1982
5	Mello-Kings	Tonite, Tonite	1957
6	Dion & the Belmonts	I Wonder Why	1958
7	Frankie Lymon & the Teenagers	Why Do Fools Fall In Love	1956
8	Channels	The Closer You Are	1956
9	Capris	There's A Moon Out	1960
10	Dubs	Chapel Of Dreams	1958
11	Flamingos	I Only Have Eyes For You	1959
12	Harptones	A Sunday Kind Of Love	1953
13	Velvets	Tonight (Could Be The	1961

		The Night	
14	Channels	That's My Desire	1957
15	Chantels	Maybe	1958
16	Earls	I Believe	1964
17	Chimes	Once In A While	1960
18	Frankie Lymon & the Teenagers	Share	1956
19	Duprees	You Belong To Me	1962
20	Danleers	One Summer Night	1958
21	Charts	Desiree	1957
22	Harptones	The Shrine Of St. Ceclia	1957
23	Moonglows	Most Of All	1955
24	Skyliners	This I Swear	1959
25	Heartbeats	Crazy For You	1955
26	Crests	Sixteen Candles	1958
27	Flamingos	Golden Teardrops	1953
28	Channels	My Love For You Will Never Die	1957
29	Crests	My Juanita	1957
30	Schooboys	Please Say You Want Me	1957
31	Valentines	Don't Say Goodbye	1957
32	Dubs	Don't Ask Me To Be Lonely	1957
33	Sonny Til & the Orioles	Crying In The Chapel	1953
34	Admirations	The Bells Of Rosa Rita	1959
35	Fascinators	Chapel Bells	1958
36	Edsels	Rama Lama Ding Dong	1961
37	Excellents	Coney Island Baby	1962
38	Jive Five	What Time Is It	1962
39	Rays	Silhouettes	1957
40	Dubs	Could This Be Magic	1957
41	Eternals	Babalu's Wedding Day	1959
42	Del Vikings	Come Go With Me	1957
43	Skyliners	Since I Don't Have You	1959
44	Diamonds	Little Darlin'	1957
45	Five Keys	Out Of Sight, Out Of Mind	1956
46	Del Vikings	Whispering Bells	1957
47	Solitaires	The Angels Sang	1956

48	Earls	Remember Then	1962
49	Harptones	That's The Way It Goes	1956
50	Jesters	The Wind	1960
51	Five Discs	Never Let You Go	1962
52	Heartbeats	Your Way	1956
53	Platters	Only You	1955
54	Norman Fox & the Rob Roys	Tell My Why	1957
55	Passions	This Is My Love	1960
56	Vito & the Salutations	Unchained Mleody	1963
57	Moonglows	Sincerely	1954
58	Students	I'm So Young	1958
59	Passions	Just To Be With You	1959
60	Paradons	Diamonds And Pearls	1960
61	Five Discs	I Remember	1958
62	Paragons	Florence	1957
63	Duprees	My Own True Love	1962
64	Earls	Never	1963
65	Crests	Step By Step	1960
66	Harptones	Three Wishes	1956
67	Cadillacs	Gloria	1954
68	Vito & the Salutations	Gloria	1962
69	Avalons	My Heart's Desire	1958
70	Jacks	Why Don't You Write Me	1955
71	Videos	Trickle, Trickle	1958
72	Six-Teens	A Casual Look	1956
73	Dells	Oh, What A Night	1956
74	Skyliners	Pennies From Heaven	1960
75	Heartbeats	A Thousand Miles Away	1956
76	Diablos	The Wind	1954
77	Monotones	Book Of Love	1958
78	Five Satins	To The Aisle	1957
79	Three Chuckles	Runaround	1954
80	Solitaires	Walking Along	1957
81	Lee Andrews & the Hearts	Teardrops	1957

82	Dreamlovers	When We Get Married	1961
83	Jaguars	The Way You Look Tonight	1956
84	Elegants	Little Star	1958
85	Cleftones	Can't We Be Sweethearts	1956
86	Demensions	Over The Rainbow	1960
87	Knockouts	Darling Lorraine	1959
88	Silhouettes	Get A Job	1957
89	Clusters	Darling Can't You Tell	1958
90	Students	Every Day Of The Week	1958
91	Timetones	Pretty, Pretty Girl	1961
92	Shep & the Limelites	Daddy's Home	1961
93	Blue Jays	Lover's Island	1961
94	Turbans	When You Dance	1954
95	Harptones	Life Is But A Dream	1954
96	Earls	Life Is But A Dream	1961
97	Three Friends	Blanche	1956
98	Cleftones	You Baby You	1956
99	Spaniels	Goodnight Sweetheart	1954
100	Velours	Can I Come Over Tonight	1957
101	Chords	Sh-Boom	1954

The U.G.H.A.'s Official Top 100 Vocal Group Recordings, 1996-2000

Finally we present a poll taken by members of the U.G.H.A. (United in Group Harmony Association) over the course of five years (1996-2000).[15] The organization was synonymous with its founder and president, Ronnie Italiano. Founded in 1976, it had roughly 2000 members,

----

[15] The tabulatiion of the Top 500 was done by member Rich Kriz using a computerized point system.

all of whom were quite serious about their music. Monthly concerts were held in northern New Jersey, and many of the old time groups, some with only one original member, got the acclaim that they didn't receive during the doo-wop era. As the population of purists aged, Ronnie lost his soap box, a two-hour weekly radio show on public radio, contracted cancer and passed away in 2008. Sadly, U.G.H.A. died when Ronnie did, and despite valiant efforts by his widow, his beloved Clifton Music music store closed as well.

The poll tallied the Top 500 songs, but since members are purists, some of their choices are really obscure. We've chosen to present their Top 100. In some ways, the results are similar to our Top 1000, in that their top groups (Harptones, Flamingos, Orioles, Heartbeats, Moonglows, Five Keys, Ravens, Cadillacs, Dominoes, Solitaires, Spaniels and Drifters) are consistent with ours.

The differences are that their favorites are older (only one song from the 1960s), less white (the first white group record, "That's My Desire" by the Belmonts appears at # 43 and the list contains only 8.4% songs by white groups, and the first female group record, "Maybe" by the Chantels, appears at #91. Female groups placed only 12 songs on their list of 500 (2.4%). By contrast, our Top 1000 has 24.6% of songs from the 1960s, approximately 14% of groups are white or white-led, and 8.2% of our groups are all female or female-led. Perhaps the most noteworthy difference is that although our list of 1000 songs has approximately 40% uptempo numbers, the U.G.H.A. list has only 5 jump tunes in their first 100, or 5% of the total, leaving 95% as ballads. Their Top 100 consists of:

THE UNITED IN GROUP HARMONY
ASSOCIATION'S

OFFICIAL TOP 500 VOCAL GROUP RECORDINGS

THE HARPTONES

Top Group With Most Selections on the Survey

Voted by the U.G.H.A.Membership   1996-2000

1	Flamingos	Golden Teardrops	1953
2	Larks	My Reverie	1951
3	Heartbeats	Crazy For You	1955
4	Harptones	A Sunday Kind Of Love	1953
5	Orioles	It's Too Soon To Know	1948
6	Teenagers	Share	1956
7	Moonglows	Most Of All	1955
8	Diablos	The Wind	1954
9	Harptones	I'll Never Tell	1953
10	Channels	The Closer You Are	1956

11	Penguins	Earth Angel	1954
12	Spaniels	You Gave Me Peace Of Mind	1956
13	Five Satins	In The Still Of The Nite	1956
14	Heartbeats	Your Way	1956
15	Five Keys	My Saddest Hour	1953
16	Heartbeats	A Thousand Miles Away	1956
17	Cadillacs	Gloria	1954
18	Mastertones	Tell Me	1954
19	Harptones	Life Is But A Dream	1955
20	Solitaires	Please Remember My Heart	1954
21	Harptones	That's The Way It Goes	1956
22	Hideaways	Can't Help Loving That Girl Of Mine	1956
23	Velours	Can I Come Over Tonight	1957
24	Moonglows	Sincerely	1954
25	Dubs	Could This Be Magic	1957
26	Students	My Vow To You	1958
27	Charts	Desiree	1957
28	Drifters	What'Cha Gonna Do	1955
29	Flamingos	Dream Of A Lifetime	1954
30	Harptones	My Memories Of You	1954
31	Lee Andrews & the Hearts	Teardrops	1957
32	Flamingos	I Only Have Eyes For You	1959
33	Heartbeats	Tormented	1955
34	Bluenotes	My Hero	1960
35	Cardinals	Shouldn't I Know	1951
36	Swallows	Dearest	1951
37	Orioles	A Kiss And A Rose	1949
38	Orioles	Crying In The Chapel	1953
39	Nutmegs	Story Untold	1955
40	Ravens	Lilacs In The Rain	1951
41	Five Keys	Red Sails In The Sunset	1952
42	Moonglows	Secret Love	1954
43	Belmonts	That's My Desire	1960
44	Esquires	Only The Angels Know	1957

45	Skyliners	Since I Don't Have You	1959
46	Spaniels	Let's Make Up	1954
47	Dubs	Don't Ask Me To Be Lonely	1957
48	Shepherds	Island Of Love	1959
49	Checkers	Nights Curtains	1952
50	Flamingos	I'll Be Home	1955
51	Little Did I Dream	Twilighters	1955
52	Superiors	Lost Love	1957
53	Castelles	My Girl Awaits Me	1953
54	Capris	God Only Knows	1954
55	Duprees	You Belong To Me	1962
56	Dell-Vikings	Come Go With Me	1956
57	Dells	Oh What A Nite	1956
58	Passions	This Is My Love	1960
59	Pearls	Tree In The Meadow	1956
60	Jesters	The Wind	1960
61	El Dorados	At My Front Door	1955
62	Continentals	Dear Lord	1956
63	Heartbeats	I Won't Be The Fool Anymore	1957
64	Students	I'm So Young	1958
65	Channels	That's My Desire	1957
66	Dominoes	These Foolish Things	1953
67	Flamingos	Lovers Never Say Goodbye	1958
68	Ravens	A Simple Prayer	1956
69	Jacks	Why Don't You Write Me	1955
70	Five Blue Notes	The Beat Of Our Hearts	1954
71	Clovers	Blue Velvet	1955
72	Charmers	I Was Wrong	1954
73	Moonglows	When I'm With You	1959
74	Dion & the Belmonts	I Wonder Why	1958
75	Drifters	Your Promise To Be Mine	1956
76	Orioles	At Night	1950
77	Avalons	Heart's Desire	1958
78	Jive Five	My True Story	1961
79	Danleers	One Summer Night	1958
80	Little Anthony &	Tears On My Pillow	1958

Imperials

81	Solitaires	The Angels Sang	1956
82	Dominoes	Do Something For Me	1950
83	Rivieras	Midnight Cocktails	1960
84	Schoolboys	Please Say You Want Me	1956
85	Solitaires	Wonder Why	1954
86	Whispers	Are You Sorry	1955
87	Fascinators	Chapel Bells	1958
88	Swallows	Eternally	1951
89	Flamingos	I Was Such A Fool	1959
90	Jaguars	The Way You Look Tonight	1956
91	Chantels	Maybe	1957
92	Swallows	Beside You	1952
93	Vibranaires	Doll Face	1954
94	Solitaires	I Don't Stand A Ghost Of A Chance	1955
95	Flamingos	A Kiss From Your Lips	1956
96	Channels	My Love For You Will Never Die	1958
97	Teenagers	Why Do Fools Fall In Love	1955
98	Five Keys	Close Your Eyes	1955
99	Channels	The Gleam In Your Eyes	1956
100	Lee Andrews/Hearts	Maybe You'll Be There	1954

Our Representative TOP 100 Songs

Before we reveal our whole list, we selected what we feel are 100 of the best songs, balanced by slow/fast and paleo-/classical/neo- categories. We chose 10% of the Top 1000, or 100 songs. But we chose these songs in an unusual way by maintaining the ratios, in terms of style and tempo, of the original 1000. By combining medium tempo songs with fast songs, the results required that we find (after rounding off):

23 songs that are Slow and Paleo-Doo-Wop
4 songs that are Fast and Paleo-Doo-Wop
27 songs that are Slow and Classical-Doo-Wop
25 songs that are Fast and Classical-Doo-Wop
9 songs that are Slow and Neo-Doo-Wop
12 songs that are Fast and Neo-Doo-Wop

Notice that the sum of songs is 100, representing 10% of the original Top 1000. It is to be noted that the same biases that led to the choosing of the Top 1000 resulted in winnowing down the total to 100. Alphabetized by group, they are:

Belmonts, Dion & the	I Wonder Why
Blue Jays	Lover's Island
Bonnevilles	Zu Zu
Bop Chords	Castle In The Sky
Cadillacs	Gloria
Cadillacs	Speedoo
Capris	There's A Moon Out Tonight
Castelles	My Girl Awaits Me
Channels (Earl Lewis &)	The Closer You Are
Charts	Zoop
Charts	Desiree
Chesters	The Fires Burn No More

Chimes	Once In A While
Classics	Til Then
Cleftones	Little Girl Of Mine
Clovers	Yes Sir, That's My Baby
Collegians	Zoom Zoom Zoom
Columbus Pharaohs	Give Me Your Love
Continentals	Dear Lord
Continentals	Fine Fine Frame
Crests	My Juanita
Crows	Gee
Danleers	One Summer Night
Del Vikings	Come Go With Me
Dells	Oh What A Night
Desires	I Wanna Rendezvous With You
Diablos	The Wind
Dion (w/Del Satins)	Runaround Sue
Diplomats (Dino &)	Hushabye My Love
Dominoes	Harbor Lights
Dominoes	Sixty Minute Man
Drifters	Someday You'll Want Me To Want You
Du Mauriers	All Night Long
Dubs	Don't Ask Me (To Be Lonely)
Duprees	You Belong To Me
Earls	Remember Then
Edsels	Rama Lama Ding Dong
El Dorados	Bim Bam Boom
Elegants	Little Star
Essentials (Billy &)	Maybe You'll Be There
Eternals	Babalu's Wedding Day
Fascinators	Oh Rose Marie
Fascinators	Chapel Bells
Fiestas	Last Night I Dreamed
Five Blue Notes	The Beat Of Our Hearts
Five Discs	Never Let You Go
Five Keys	Red Sails In The Sunset
Five Satins	I Remember (In The Still Of The Night)

Flamingos	Golden Teardrops
Flamingos	I Only Have Eyes For You
Flips (Little Joey &)	Bongo Stomp
Harptones	A Sunday Kind Of Love
Heartbeats	Crazy For You
Hearts (Lee Andrews &)	Long Lonely Nights
Hollywood Flames	Buzz Buzz Buzz
Imaginations	Mystery Of You
Impalas	Sorry (I Ran All The Way Home)
Imperials	Tears On My Pillow
Jaguars	The Way You Look Tonight
Jesters	Love No One But You
Jive Five	My True Story
Juniors (Danny &)	At The Hop
Larks	My Reverie
Love Notes	United
Marcels	Blue Moon
Marcels	Goodbye To Love
Meadowlarks (Don Julian &)	Heaven And Paradise
Mello-Kings	Tonight Tonight
Mellows (Lillian Leach &)	Smoke From Your Cigarette
Monotones	Book Of Love
Moonglows	Most Of All
Mystics	Hushabye
Mystics	Darling I Know Now
Nutmegs	Ship Of Love
Orchids	Newly Wed
Orioles	What Are You Doing New Year's Eve
Paragons	Let's Start All Over Again
Passions	I Only Want You
Penguins	Hey Senorita
Penguins	Earth Angel
Platters	My Prayer
Quinns	Hong Kong
Quotations	Ala-Men-Sa-Aye
Ravens	Count Every Star
Rob Roys (Norman Fox &)	Tell My Why

Salutations (Vito &)	Unchained Melody
Schoolboys	Please Say You Want Me
Shells	Baby Oh Baby
Silhouettes	Get A Job
Solitaires	Please Remember My Heart
Solitaires	I Really Love You So (Honey Babe)
Spaniels	Goodnight, Sweethear, Goodnight
Students	I'm So Young
Swallows	Since You've Been Away
Swallows	It Ain't The Meat
Teenagers (F. Lymon &)	Why Do Fools Fall In Love
Tokens	Tonight I Fell In Love
Turbans	When You Dance
Videos	Trickle Trickle
Zodiacs (M. Williams &)	Stay

Describing the Top 1000

It should be obvious that the choices for the tracks listed below are personal and involve biases. All we can do is lay them out for the reader. We grew up in New York city, and have an affinity for that sound. We're not alone in that feeling since the New York sound (which includes New Jersey and parts of Connecticut) led the way in quantity of output and arguably in terms of quality as well.

The senior author's first large exposure to doo-wop occurred during the revival of 1961, when the "Oldies But Goodies" series by Art Laboe let us grind to the "Big Three" of doo-wop standards: "In The Still of The Night," "Earth Angel" and "Tonight, Tonight" (among others), which became more popular than when they were first released in the mid-1950s. In 1961, at the age of 15, we all loved the old popular slow songs, but for fast songs gravitated to the Neo-doo-wop sounds of the Earls, Marcels and Five Discs. Earlier, in the 1950s, we listened to Chuck Berry, Elvis Presley, and Jerry Lee Lewis and Little Richard as well as popular music

The journey of these authors through the world of doo-wop was serpentine and changed focus many times. First was a two year long study of the field that produced "Doo-Wop: The Forgotten Third of Rock 'n' Roll,"[16] which made the argument that, compared with rhythm & blues and rockabilly, doo-wop "got no respect." At the time both of us were listening to WCBS-FM radio which, under the auspices of first Norm N. Nite and then Don K. Reed serenaded us for five hours every Sunday night in New York. The "Doo-Wop Shop" (and the "Nite Train Show" before it) had a large audience and spun the most popular doo-wop oldies.

---

[16] Gribin, Anthony J. & Schiff, Matthew M. The Forgotten Third of Rock 'n' Roll. Krause Publications, Iola, WI: 1992.

"The Forgotten Third" was published in 1992. Being invited to appear on close to a dozen different radio shows, including Don K. Reed's, we stumbled upon a whole new underground world of doo-wop, except you couldn't call it that. This world was centered around an organization called the "United in Group Harmony Association" (UGHA), based in New Jersey and headed by a guy named Ronnie Italiano. Its members were purists, abandoned the term "doo-wop" in favor of "rhythm & blues" and/or "vocal group harmony," and looked down on those who balked at the change.

To the purist, doo-wop represented later (meaning 1960s), whiter and less well-sung music. "Ronnie I" as he was universally known, stated that white groups couldn't sing as well as black groups and that female groups were second class because they didn't have the range of voices that male groups displayed. (In a poll of UGHA members, conducted by an oldies store called the Relic Rack in 1992 of the Top 152 groups, the first white group, the Skyliners, came in at number 52 and the first female group, the Chantels, placed 99th.)

Being older, Ronnie I was "imprinted" with earlier, slower and blacker sounds. Ronnie was not at all prejudiced, and his holding a radically different view of the music than we did was a wonderful experience and an education. We joined UGHA, attended their concerts, and drilled deeper into the music we loved. And it led to an appreciation for those older, slower and blacker sounds.

A second education came with during the development of the second book, "The Complete Book of Doo-Wop."[17] This work included chapters on the "Doo-Wopolitics" and "Doo-Wogeography." To help with the geography section, we enlisted six guys to discuss the different sounds of different parts of the country and to give their 50 local favorites. They were Ronnie I for the

---

[17] Gribin, Anthony J. & Schiff, Matthew M. The Complete Book of Doo-Wop Krause Publications, Iola, WI: 2000.

New York sound, Bob Pruter for Chicago, Nay Nasser for Washington/Baltimore, Gordon Skadberg for the Southern Sound, Bob Bosco for Philadelphia and Steve Propes for Los Angeles. Once more, we learned something important. We knew all the most popular songs from these far-flung places, but the guest experts gave us another "drilling down" experience. Again, we were grateful for the education.

Getting back to the Top 1000 list, we believe it is fairly representative of the best of the best. Sheer numbers help. If we had published a Top 10, and asked 100 doo-wop lovers to do the same, there would have been little overlap among the raters. But with 1000 choices, we are guessing that just about all 100 would agree on a core group of the top songs, including the "Big Three," "I Wonder Why" by Dion & the Belmonts and "Crying in the Chapel" by Sonny Til & the Orioles, as examples. Everyone's choices will vary with their age, gender, race and preference for slow or fast music.

Statistics for our Top 1000 appear below.

	Paleo	Classical	Neo	Sum
Slow	230	270	85	585
Medium	1	6	17	24
Fast	43	245	103	391
Sum	274	521	205	1000

Almost 60% of the Top 1000 are slow songs. 27% are Paleo-Doo-Wop, that is came out (predominantly) in or before 1954. 52% are Classical Doo-Wop, stemming from 1955 to 1959 and 21% are Neo-Doo-Wop, appearing in 1960 or after.

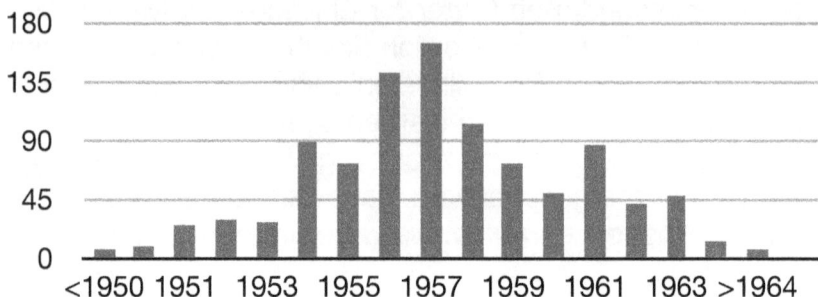

The reader will notice what in statistics is called a bi-modal (two peaks) distribution, the first high point occurring in 1957 (Classical) and the second in 1961 (Neo-). 494 groups are represented in the list, counting the Belmonts and Dion & the Belmonts as separate groups, but the Diablos and Nolan Strong & the Diablos as the same. There are 336 separate labels which issued these songs. Second or third labels were not counted.

The Drifters (B), the group featuring Clyde McPhatter, was most represented with 13 songs. The Platters placed 12, the Five Keys, Flamingos and Solitaires 11. The Dominoes, Harptones and Cadillacs had 10. The Clovers, Heartbeats, Moonglows, Nutmegs, Orioles, Lee Andrews & the Hearts, and Frankie Lymon & the Teenagers placed 9. The Crests, Ravens and Spaniels, Cleftones and Jesters were represented 8 times. The Channels, Coasters, Paragons, Shirelles and Swallows had 7. The Earls, El Dorados, Five Satins, Four Fellows, and Little Anthony & the Imperials placed 6. Finally, the Crows, Arthur Lee Maye & the Crowns, Continentals, Dion & the Belmonts, Charts, Cardinals, Castelles, Charms, Dells, Diablos, Dubs, Five Discs, Four Buddies, Larks (A), Mellows, Mystics, Norman Fox & the Rob Roys, Skyliners, Bop-Chords, Dell Vikings, Spiders and Lewis Lymon & the Teenchords place 5.

These 52 groups account for 366 of the Top 1000 Hits. Seven of the 52 are predominantly white (13.5%), 42 are black (86.5%). One group was all female, another had a female lead (3.8% combined). 44 of the 1000 songs are performed by all-female groups (4.4%) and another 38 (3.8%) feature female leads with predominantly male groups. That leaves 918 songs by mostly male groups (91.8%). For the reader, these numbers should make clear the biases of these authors.

How to Read and Use the Top 1000 Checklist

Each entry has a box and a circle next to it. The box can be checked if you "have" the track in question. The circle can be checked if you've heard the track. Or perhaps if the track is on your "want" or "need" list. There is space at the bottom of each page for your own notes, ratings, comments or complaints. If there are songs that the reader thinks should've been included, but weren't, the authors would like to hear from you.

Key:

FP= Fast tempo and Paleo-Doo-Wop
MP= Medium tempo and Paleo-Doo-Wop
SP= Slow tempo and Paleo-Doo-Wop
FC= Fast tempo and Classical Doo-Wop
MC= Medium tempo and Classical Doo-Wop
SC= Slow tempo and Classical Doo-Wop
FN= Fast tempo and Neo-Doo-Wop
MN= Medium tempo and Neo-Doo-Wop
SN= Slow tempo and Neo-Doo-Wop
GG= (all) girl group
GL= girl lead, male group
100= in the Top 100

Warning! This list is for the personal use and pleasure of authorized readers only. It may not be copied, distributed for profit or taken in vain; if you choose, however, it may be memorized at your own risk.

The Top 1000 Doo-Wop Songs

| □○ Academics | Something Cool | 1958 | FC |

Academics

Adelphis

| □○ Adelphis | Kathleen | 1958 | FC |

| □○ Admirations | The Bells Of Rosa Rita | 1959 | SC |

Admirations

Chuck Alaimo Quartet

| □○ Alaimo Quartet, The Chuck | How I Love You | 1957 | SC |

| □○ Alley Cats | Puddin' 'N 'Tain | 1962 | FN |

Alley Cats

Angels (A), Sonny Gordon & the

| □○ Ambassadors | Darling I'm Sorry | 1954 | SP |

| □○ Angels (A), Sonny Gordon & the | Wedding Bells Are Ringing My Ears | 1954 | SP |

☐○ Angels (B)	Til	1961	SN/FG
☐○ Angels (B)	My Boyfriend's Back	1963	FN/FG

Angels (B)

Aquatones

☐○ Aquatones	You	1958	SC/FG
☐○ Arrogants	Mirror Mirror	1963	FN

Arrogants

Pepe & the Astros

☐○ Astros, Pepe & the	Judy My Love (Judy Mi Amor)	1961	FN
☐○ Audios, Cell Foster & the	I Prayed For You	1956	SC
☐○ Avalons	My Heart's Desire	1958	SC
☐○ Avons	Our Love Will Never End	1956	FC
☐○ Avons	Baby	1957	SC

Avalons

Avons

□ ○ Aztecs, Jose & the   My Aching Heart   1955   SC

□ ○ Bachelors (Dean   Baby   1955   FC
     Barlow & the)

Jose & the Aztecs

Bachelors, Dean Barlow & the

□ ○ Baltineers   Moments Like This   1956   SP

□ ○ Baltineers   Tears In My Eyes   1956   SP

□ ○ Bel-Larks   A Million And One Dreams   1963   SN

Bell Notes

Bel-Larks

□○ Bell Notes	I've Had It	1959	FC
□○ Belmonts	Diddle De-Dum	1962	FN
□○ Belmonts (Dion & the)	Don't Pity Me	1958	SC
□○ Belmonts (Dion & the)	I Wonder Why	1958	FC

Dion & the Belmonts   *Belmonts*

□○ Belmonts (Dion & the)	No One Knows	1958	SC
□○ Belmonts (Dion & the)	A Teenager In Love	1959	FC
□○ Belmonts (Dion & the)	Where Or When	1960	SC
□○ Belvin, Jesse (& group)	Goodnight My Love	1956	SC

Jesse Belvin

Blenders

□○ Bing Bongs (Dicky Dell & the)	Ding-A-Ling A-Ling-Ding-Dong	1958	FC

☐○ Bishops	The Wedding	1961	SN
☐○ Blenders	The Masquerade Is Over	1950	SP
☐○ Blenders	I'd Be A Fool Again	1952	SP

Blue Jays

Patti LaBelle & the Blue Belles

☐○ Blue Belles (Patti LaBelle & the)	You'll Never Walk Alone	1963	SN /FG
☐○ Blue Jays	Let's Make Love	1961	SN
☐○ Blue Jays	Lover's Island	1961	SN
☐○ Blue Jeans (Bobb B. Soxx & the)	Why Do Lovers Break Each Others Hearts	1963	FN /FL

*Bobb B. Soxx
Blue Jeans*

Bob Knight Four

| ☐○ Blue Notes | If You Love Me | 1956 | SN |
| ☐○ Blue Notes | My Hero | 1960 | SN |

□ ○ Blue Notes	Blue Star		1961	SN
□ ○ Bob Knight Four	Good Goodbye		1961	SC
□ ○ Bobbettes	Mr. Lee		1957	FC /FG

Bobbettes

Bonnie Sisters

□ ○ Bonnevilles	Lorraine		1960	SC
□ ○ Bonnevilles	Zu Zu		1960	SC
□ ○ Bonnie Sisters	Cry Baby		1956	FC /FG
□ ○ Bop Chords	Castle In The Sky		1957	FC
□ ○ Bop Chords	I Really Love You		1957	SC
□ ○ Bop Chords	My Darling To You		1957	SC

Bop Chords

□ ○ Bop Chords	So Why		1957	FC
□ ○ Bop Chords	When I Woke Up This Morning	1957	FC

□○ Bosstones	Mope-itty Mope	1959	FN
□○ Buccaneers	Dear Ruth	1953	SP
□○ C-Notes (aka C-Tones)	On Your Mark	1957	FC
□○ Cabineers	Each Time	1951	SP

Cabineers

Cadets

□○ Cadets	Fools Rush In	1956	FC
□○ Cadets	Stranded In The Jungle	1956	FC
□○ Cadillacs	Gloria	1954	SP

Cadillacs

| □○ Cadillacs | I Wonder Why | 1954 | SP |
| □○ Cadillacs | Wishing Well | 1954 | SP |

□ ○ Cadillacs	Down The Road	1955	FP
□ ○ Cadillacs	Speedoo	1955	FP
□ ○ Cadillacs	Sympathy	1955	SP
□ ○ Cadillacs	The Girl I Love	1956	FP
□ ○ Cadillacs	You Are	1956	SP
□ ○ Cadillacs	Zoom	1956	FP
□ ○ Cadillacs	My Girl Friend	1957	FP
□ ○ Calvanes	Don't Take Your Love From Me	1955	SC

Calvanes

Camelots

| □ ○ Camelots (aka Cupids/Harps) | Don't Leave Me Baby | 1964 | FC |
| □ ○ Candles (Rochell & the) | Once Upon A Time | 1960 | SN |

Rochell & the Candles

Cap-Tans

□○ Candles (Rochell & the)	Each Night	1962	SN
□○ Cap-Tans	I'm So Crazy For Love	1950	SP
□○ Cap-Tans	With All My Love	1950	SP
□○ Capistranos (John Littleton & the)	Now Darling	1958	SC
□○ Capris (A)	God Only Knows	1954	SP /FL
□○ Capris (A)	It Was Moonglow	1954	SP /FL

Capris (A)

Capris (B)

□○ Capris (B)	There's A Moon Out Tonight	1958	SN
□○ Capris (B)	Where I Fell In Love	1961	SN
□○ Capris (B)	Morse Code Of Love	1982	FN
□○ Cardinals	Shouldn't I Know	1951	SP

Cardinals

□ ○ Cardinals	Wheel Of Fortune	1952	SP
□ ○ Cardinals	You Are My Only Love	1953	SP
□ ○ Cardinals	Under A Blanket Of Blue	1954	SP
□ ○ Cardinals	The Door Is Still Open	1955	SP
□ ○ Cardinals	Off Shore	1956	SP
□ ○ Carnations (aka Startones)	Long Tall Girl	1961	FC
□ ○ Carollons (Lonnie & the)	Chapel Of Tears	1960	SN

Lonnie & the Carollons

Caslons

□ ○ Carousels	You Can Come (If You Want To)	1961	SN /FG
□ ○ Caslons	Anniversary Of Love	1961	FN
□ ○ Castelles	My Girls Awaits Me	1953	SP

Castelles

Castells

□ ○ Castelles	Do You Remember	1954	SP

□ ○ Castelles	Over A Cup Of Coffee	1954	SP
□ ○ Castelles	This Silver Ring	1954	SP
□ ○ Castelles	Heavenly Father	1955	SP
□ ○ Castells	So This Is Love	1962	SN
□ ○ Castro, Vince (with the Tonettes)	Bong Bong (I Love You Madly)	1958	FC

Vince Castro & the Tonettes

Cavaliers

□ ○ Castroes	Dearest Darling	1959	SC
□ ○ Cavaliers	Dance Dance Dance	1958	FC
□ ○ Cavaliers	The Magic Age Of Sixteen	1963	SN
□ ○ Cellos	Rang Tang Ding Dong (I Am the Japanese Sandman)	1957	FC

Cellos

Chandeliers Quintet

| □ ○ Cellos | You Took My Love | 1957 | SC |

□ ○ Chalets	Fat Fat Mommio	1961	FC
□ ○ Chandeliers (aka Chandeliers Quintet)	Blueberry Sweet	1958	FC
□ ○ Chandler, Gene (w/Dukays)	Duke Of Earl	1961	MN

Channels   *Dukays*

□ ○ Channels (Earl Lewis & the)	Now You Know (I Love You So)	1956	FC
□ ○ Channels (Earl Lewis & the)	The Closer You Are	1956	SC
□ ○ Channels (Earl Lewis & the)	The Gleam In Your Eyes	1956	SC
□ ○ Channels (Earl Lewis & the)	Bye Bye Baby	1957	FC
□ ○ Channels (Earl Lewis & the)	Flames In My Heart	1957	SC
□ ○ Channels (Earl Lewis & the)	My Love Will Never Die	1957	SC
□ ○ Channels (Earl Lewis & the)	That's My Desire	1957	SC
□ ○ Chantels	He's Gone	1957	SC /FG

□ ○ Chantels	Maybe	1958	SC /FG
□ ○ Chantels	Look In My Eyes	1961	SC /FG

Chantels

Chanters

□ ○ Chanters	Angel Darling	1958	SC
□ ○ Chanters	I Need Your Tenderness	1958	SC
□ ○ Chanters	My My Darling	1958	FC
□ ○ Chanters	No No No	1958	FC

Chaperones

Charades

□ ○ Chaperones	Cruise To The Moon	1960	SN
□ ○ Charades	Please Be My Love Tonight	1963	SN

□ ○ Chariots	Gloria	1959	SC
□ ○ Charles, Jimmy (w/Revelettes)	A Million To One	1960	SN
□ ○ Charms (Otis & the Charms)	Ivory Tower	1954	SC
□ ○ Charms (Otis & the Charms)	My Baby Dearest Darling	1954	FC
□ ○ Charms (Otis & the Charms)	Two Hearts	1954	FC
□ ○ Charms (Otis & the Charms)	Gumdrop	1956	FC
□ ○ Charms (Otis & the Charms)	One Night Only	1956	FC

Otis Williams & the Charms

Charts

□ ○ Charts	Dance Girl	1957	FC
□ ○ Charts	Desiree	1957	SC
□ ○ Charts	Why Do You Cry	1957	SC
□ ○ Charts	You're The Reason	1957	SC
□ ○ Charts	Zoop	1957	FC

□ ○ Checkers	Nights Curtains	1952	SP
□ ○ Checkers	Ghost Of My Baby	1953	SP
□ ○ Checkers	White Cliffs Of Dover	1954	FP

Checkers

Chesters

□ ○ Cherokees	My Heavenly Angel	1961	FN
□ ○ Chesters	The Fires Burn No More	1958	SC
□ ○ Chestnuts	Love Is True	1956	SC /FL

Chestnuts

Chevrons

| □ ○ Chevrons | Lullabye | 1959 | FC |
| □ ○ Chex (Tex & the) | I Do Love You | 1961 | SN |

Tex & the Chex

Chiffons

□ ○ Chiffons	He's So Fine	1963	FN /FG
□ ○ Chiffons	I Have A Boyfriend	1963	FN /FG
□ ○ Chiffons	Oh My Lover	1963	FN /FG
□ ○ Chiffons	One Fine Day	1963	FN /FG
□ ○ Chimes	Once In A While	1960	SN
□ ○ Chimes	I'm In The Mood For Love	1961	SN

Chimes

Chips

□ ○ Chips	Oh, My Darlin'	1956	SC
□ ○ Chips	Rubber Biscuit	1956	FC
□ ○ Chords	Sh-Boom	1954	FP

Kool Gents & Dee Clark
(bot. rt.)

Chords

□ ○ Clark, Dee (bb the Kool Gents) Just Like A Fool 1960 SC

□ ○ Classic IV Island Of Paradise 1962 SN

Classic IV

Classics

□ ○ Classics Till Then 1963 SN

□ ○ Clefs We Three 1952 SP

Clefs

Cleftones

□ ○ Cleftones	Can't We Be Sweethearts?	1956	FC
□ ○ Cleftones	Little Girl Of Mine	1956	FC
□ ○ Cleftones	String Around My Heart	1956	FC
□ ○ Cleftones	String Around My Heart	1956	FC
□ ○ Cleftones	You Baby You	1956	FC
□ ○ Cleftones	See You Next Year	1957	SC
□ ○ Cleftones	Why You Do Me Like You Do	1957	FC
□ ○ Cleftones	Heart And Soul	1961	MN
□ ○ Click-Ettes	Lover's Prayer	1960	SN /FG

Click-Ettes

Cliques

□ ○ Cliques	Girl In My Dreams	1956	SC
□ ○ Clovers	Yes Sir, That's My Baby	1950	SP
□ ○ Clovers	Fool, Fool, Fool	1951	FP
□ ○ Clovers	Needless	1951	SP
□ ○ Clovers	Skylark	1951	SP
□ ○ Clovers	I Played The Fool	1952	SP
□ ○ Clovers	One Mint Julep	1952	FP

Clovers

Clusters

□ ○ Clovers	Blue Velvet	1955	SP
□ ○ Clovers	Devil Or Angel	1956	SP
□ ○ Clovers	Love Potion No. 9	1959	FC
□ ○ Clusters	Darling Can't You Tell	1958	FC
□ ○ Coasters	Down In Mexico	1956	FC
□ ○ Coasters	Searchin'	1957	MC
□ ○ Coasters	Young Blood	1957	FC
□ ○ Coasters	Yakety Yak	1958	FC
□ ○ Coasters	Along Came Jones	1959	FC
□ ○ Coasters	Charlie Brown	1959	FC
□ ○ Coasters	Poison Ivy	1959	FC

Coasters

145

□○ Cobras	La La	1964	FN

Cobras

Colts

□○ Coins	Blue, Can't Get No Place With You	1954	FC
□○ Collegians	Zoom Zoom Zoom	1957	FC
□○ Collegians	Heavenly Night	1958	SC
□○ Collegians	Let's Go For A Ride	1958	FC
□○ Colts	Adorable	1955	FC
□○ Columbus Pharaohs	Give Me Your Love	1957	SC

Columbus Pharaohs

Consorts

□○ Concords	Candlelight	1954	SP
□○ Consorts	Please Be Mine	1961	FN
□○ Contenders	The Clock	1963	FN

Contenders

Continentals

□ ○ Continentals	Dear Lord	1956	SC
□ ○ Continentals	Fine Fine Frame	1956	FC
□ ○ Continentals	Picture Of Love	1956	FC
□ ○ Continentals	Soft And Sweet	1956	SC
□ ○ Continentals	You're An Angel	1956	SC
□ ○ Convincers	Rejected Love	1962	SN

Convincers

Cookies

□ ○ Cookies	Chains	1962	FN /FG
□ ○ Cookies	Don't Say Nothin' Bad (About My Baby	1963	FN /FG
□ ○ Copasetics	Collegian	1956	FC /FL
□ ○ Cordells	The Beat Of My Heart	1961	FN

Cordells

Coronets

□ ○ Cordovans	Come On Baby	1960	FC
□ ○ Coronets	Nadine	1953	SP
□ ○ Corsairs	Smoky Places	1961	MN

Corsairs

Corvairs

□ ○ Corvairs	True True Love	1962	FN
□ ○ Cosmic Rays	Daddy's Gonna Tell You No Lies	1960	FC
□ ○ Creations	Wake Up In The Morning	1961	FC

Creations

Crescendos

| □ ○ Crescendos | Oh Julie | 1957 | SC |

148

□○ Crescents (A), Pat   Darling Come Back   1956   FC
    Cordel & the   /FL

Pat Cordel & the Crescents

Crests

□○ Crescents (B)	Everybody Knew But Me	1957	SC
□○ Crests	My Juanita	1957	FC
□○ Crests	No One To Love	1957	SC
□○ Crests	Sweetest One	1957	SC
□○ Crests	Sixteen Candles	1958	SC
□○ Crests	The Angels Listened In	1959	FC
□○ Crests	Isn't It Amazing	1960	FC
□○ Crests	Step By Step	1960	FC
□○ Crests	Trouble In Paradise	1960	FC

Dean Barlow & the Crickets

Arthur Lee Maye

□ ○ Crickets (Dean Barlow &)	You're Mine	1953	SP
□ ○ Crickets (Dean Barlow &)	Your Love	1954	SP
□ ○ Crowns (Arthur Lee Maye &)	I Wanna Love	1954	FC
□ ○ Crowns (Arthur Lee Maye &)	Love Me Always	1955	SC
□ ○ Crowns (Arthur Lee Maye &)	Truly	1955	SC
□ ○ Crowns (Arthur Lee Maye &)	Gloria	1956	SC
□ ○ Crowns (Arthur Lee Maye &)	This Is The Night For Love	1956	SC

Crows

Crystals

□ ○ Crows	Gee	1954	FP
□ ○ Crows	I Love You So	1954	SP
□ ○ Crows	Miss You	1954	SP
□ ○ Crows	Untrue	1954	SP
□ ○ Crows	Baby Doll	1955	FC
□ ○ Crystals	There's No Other (Like My	1961	SN

	Baby		/FG
□○ Crystals	He's Sure The Boy I Love	1962	FN /FG
□○ Crystals	Da Doo Ron Ron	1963	FN /FG
□○ Cuff Links	Guided Missiles	1957	SC
□○ Cupids	Brenda	1962	SN
□○ Danderliers	My Autumn Love	1955	SC

Danderliers

Danleers

□○ Danleers	One Summer Night	1958	SC
□○ Danleers	I Really Love You	1958	SC
□○ Darchaes (Ray & the)	Carol	1962	SN

Ray & the Darchaes

Del Satins

□○ Debonaires	Darling	1957	FC

□ ○ Decoys	It's Gonna Be Allright	1963	FN /FL
□ ○ Del Satins	Teardrops Follow Me	1962	FN
□ ○ Delighters (Donald Jenkins & the)	(Native Girl) Elephant Walk	1963	FN
□ ○ Dell Vikings	A Sunday Kind Of Love	1957	FC
□ ○ Dell Vikings	Come Go With Me	1957	FC
□ ○ Dell Vikings	I'm Spinning	1957	FC
□ ○ Dell Vikings	When I Come Home	1957	SC
□ ○ Dell Vikings	Whispering Bells	1957	FC

Dell Vikings

Dells

□ ○ Dells	Tell The World	1955	SC
□ ○ Dells	Oh What A Night	1956	SC
□ ○ Dells	Time Makes You Change	1957	FC
□ ○ Dells	Why Do You Have To Go	1957	SC
□ ○ Dells	Dry Your Eyes	1959	SC
□ ○ Delmonicos	World's Biggest Fool	1964	SN

Delmonicos

Reperata & the Delrons

□ ○ Delrons (Reperata & the)	Whenever A Teenager Cries	1964	SN /FG
□ ○ Delrons (Reperata & the)	Tommy	1965	SN /FG
□ ○ Delroys	Bermuda Shorts	1957	FC

Delroys

Deltairs

□ ○ Deltairs	Lullabye Of The Bells	1957	SC /FG
□ ○ Deltas	Lamplight	1957	FC
□ ○ Demens	Take Me As I Am	1957	SC

Demens

Demensions

□○ Demensions   Over The Rainbow   1962   SN

□○ Demilles   Donna Lee   1964   FN

Demilles

Desires

□○ Desires   Hey, Lena   1959   FC

□○ Desires   Let It Please Be You   1959   SC

□○ Desires   I Wanna Rendezvous With   1960   FC
                          You

□○ Devotions   Rip Van Winkle   1961   FN

Devotions

Nolan Strong & the Diablos

□○ Diablos   The Wind   1954   SP

□○ Diablos (featuring Adios My Desert Love   1954   SC
     Nolan Strong)

□○ Diablos (featuring Hold Me Until Eternity   1955   SC
     Nolan Strong)

□○ Diablos (Nolan Strong & the)	Can't We Talk This Over	1957	SC
□○ Diablos (Nolan Strong & the)	If I (Could Be With You Tonight)	1959	FC
□○ Dialtones	Til I Heard It From You	1960	FN /FL

Dialtones

Diamonds

□○ Diamonds	A Beggar For Your Kisses	1952	SP
□○ Diamonds	Cherry	1953	SP
□○ Diamonds	Two Loves Have I	1953	SP
□○ DiMucci, Dion (w/Del Satins)	Runaround Sue	1961	FN
□○ DiMucci, Dion (w/Del Satins)	Lovers Who Wander	1962	FN
□○ DiMucci, Dion (w/Del Satins)	Donna The Prima Donna	1963	FN

Dion DiMucci

Dino & the Diplomats

□○ Diplomats (Dino & the)	Hushabye My Love	1961	FN
□○ Diplomats (Dino & the)	I Can't Believe	1961	FN
□○ Dodgers	Drip Drop	1955	SP
□○ Dominoes	Do Something For Me	1950	SP
□○ Dominoes	Harbor Lights	1951	SP
□○ Dominoes	Sixty Minute Man	1951	FP
□○ Dominoes	Have Mercy Baby	1952	FP
□○ Dominoes	I'd Be Satisfied	1952	SP
□○ Dominoes	The Bells	1952	SP
□○ Dominoes	When The Swallows Come Back To Capistrano	1952	SP
□○ Dominoes	These Foolish Things	1953	SP
□○ Dominoes	Deep Purple	1957	SP
□○ Dominoes	Stardust	1957	SP

Dominoes

Don Juans

□○ Don Juans	Girl Of My Dreams	1959	SC

□ ○ Dorn, Jerry (with the Hurricanes)	Wishing Well		1956	SP
□ ○ Dovells	Bristol Stomp		1961	FN
□ ○ Dovells	No No No		1961	FN

Dovells

Miriam Grate & the Dovers

□ ○ Dovers (Miriam Grate & the)	Sweet As A Flower		1959	SC /FL
□ ○ Dovers (Miriam Grate & the)	Devil You May Be		1961	SC
□ ○ Dream Kings	More Than Yesterday, Less Than Tomorrow		1957	SC

Dream Kings

Dreamers

Dreamlovers

□ ○ Dreamers	Tears In My Eyes	1955	SC
□ ○ Dreamlovers	When We Get Married	1961	SN
□ ○ Drifters (A)	I'm The Caring Kind	1950	SP
□ ○ Drifters (B)	Money Honey	1953	FP

Drifters (B)

□ ○ Drifters (B)	The Way I Feel	1953	SP
□ ○ Drifters (B)	Honey Love	1954	FP
□ ○ Drifters (B)	Someday You'll Want Me To Want You	1954	SP
□ ○ Drifters (B)	Such A Night	1954	FP
□ ○ Drifters (B)	Warm Your Heart	1954	SP
□ ○ Drifters (B)	White Christmas	1954	FP
□ ○ Drifters (B)	Adorable	1955	SP
□ ○ Drifters (B)	What'Cha Gonna Do	1955	FP
□ ○ Drifters (B)	Ruby Baby	1956	FP
□ ○ Drifters (B)	Your Promise To Be Mine	1956	SP
□ ○ Drifters (B)	Let The Boogie Woogie Roll	1960	FP
□ ○ Drifters (B)	Sweets For My Sweet	1961	FN

☐ ○ Drifters (C)   There Goes My Baby   1959   MN

Drifters (C)   *Dubs*

☐ ○ Drifters (C)   This Magic Moment   1959   MN

☐ ○ Drifters (C)   Save The Last Dance For Me   1960   MN

☐ ○ Du Mauriers   All Night Long   1957   FC

☐ ○ Dubs   Could This Be Magic   1957   SC

☐ ○ Dubs   Don't Ask Me (To Be Lonely)   1957   SC

☐ ○ Dubs   Beside My Love   1958   SC

☐ ○ Dubs   Chapel Of Dreams   1958   SC

☐ ○ Dubs   Is There A Love For Me   1958   SC

☐ ○ Duprees   My Own True Love   1962   SN

☐ ○ Duprees   You Belong To Me   1962   SN

☐ ○ Duprees   Have Your Heard   1963   SN

☐ ○ Duprees   Why Don't You Believe Me   1963   SN

Duprees

Earls

159

□ ○ Earls	Life Is But A Dream	1961	FN
□ ○ Earls	Lookin' For My Baby	1961	FN
□ ○ Earls	Eyes	1962	FN
□ ○ Earls	Remember Then	1962	FN
□ ○ Earls	Never	1963	FN
□ ○ Earls	I Believe	1964	SN
□ ○ Ebb Tides (Nino & the)	Jukebox Saturday Night	1961	FN

Nino & the Ebb Tides

Ebonaires

□ ○ Ebonaires	Love Call	1959	SC
□ ○ Echoes (A)	Ding Dong	1957	FC
□ ○ Echoes (B)	Baby Blue	1961	FN

Echoes (B)

Edsels

□ ○ Edsels	What Brought Us Together	1960	SN
□ ○ Edsels	Rama Lama Ding Dong	1961	FC

| □○ Edsels | Shake Shake Sherry | 1962 | FN |
| □○ El Capris | Oh, But She Did | 1956 | FC |

El Domingoes

El Capris

□○ El Domingoes	Lucky Me, I'm In Love	1962	FN
□○ El Dorados	Baby I Need You	1954	SP
□○ El Dorados	At My Front Door	1955	FC
□○ El Dorados	I Began To Realize	1955	SC
□○ El Dorados	I'll Be Forever Loving You	1955	FC
□○ El Dorados	Bim Bam Boom	1956	FC
□○ El Dorados	There In The Night	1956	SP

Eldaros

El Dorados

| □○ Elchords | Peppermint Stick | 1957 | FC |
| □○ Eldaros | Please Surrender | 1958 | SC |

□ ○ Elegants	Goodnight	1958	SC
□ ○ Elegants	Little Star	1958	MC

Elegants

Embers

□ ○ Elgins	Here In Your Arms	1964	SN
□ ○ Embers	Solitaire	1961	SC
□ ○ Emblems (Patty & the)	Mixed Up, Shook Up Girl	1964	FN /FG

Patty & the Emblems

Emotions

□ ○ Emotions	Echo	1962	MN
□ ○ Encounters	Don't Stop Now	1965	FN

Encounters

Ermines

| □○ Ermines | I'm So Used To You Now | 1956 | FC |
| □○ Essentials (Billy & the) | Maybe You'll Be There | 1962 | FN |

Billy & the Essentials

Essex

□○ Essex	A Walkin' Miracle	1963	FN /FL
□○ Essex	Easier Said Than Done	1963	FN /FL
□○ Eternals	Babalu's Wedding Day	1959	FC
□○ Eternals	My Girl	1959	SC
□○ Eternals	Rockin' In The Jungle	1959	FC

Eternals

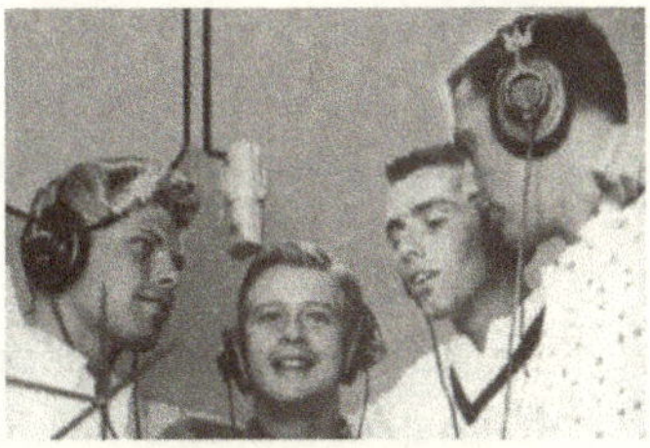

Dante & the Evergreens

| □○ Evergreens Dante & the) | Alley Oop | 1960 | FN |
| □○ Excellents | Coney Island Baby | 1962 | SN |

Excellents

Dennis & the Explorers

□ ○ Explorers   Vision Of Love   1960   SN
    (Dennis & the)

□ ○ Fabulaires   While Walking   1957   FC

Fabulaires

Fabulous
Pearl
Devines

□ ○ Fabulous Pearl   You've Been Gone   1959   FC
    Devines

□ ○ Fabulous Twilights, Village Of Love   1962   FN
    Nathaniel Mayer &

Nathaniel Mayer

Falcons

| □ ○ Falcons | You're So Fine | 1959 | FC |
| □ ○ Fantastics | There Goes My Love | 1959 | SC |

Fantastics

Fascinators (A)

□ ○ Fascinators (A)	My Beauty, My Own	1954	SP
□ ○ Fascinators (B)	Chapel Bells	1958	SC
□ ○ Fascinators (B)	Wonder Who	1958	FC
□ ○ Fascinators (B)	Oh Rose Marie	1959	FC
□ ○ Fascinators (B)	Who Do You Think You Are	1959	SC

Fascinators (B)

Fashions

| □ ○ Fashions | I'm Dreaming Of You | 1959 | FC /FL |
| □ ○ Feathers | Johnny, Darling | 1954 | SP |

| ☐ ○ Fi-Tones | Foolish Dreams | 1957 | SC |
| ☐ ○ Fi-Tones | My Faith | 1957 | SC |

Feathers

Fi-Tones

| ☐ ○ Fi-Tones Quintette | It Wasn't A Lie | 1955 | SC |
| ☐ ○ Fidelitys | The Things I Love | 1958 | SC |

Fidelitys

Fiestas

☐ ○ Fiestas	Last Night I Dreamed	1958	SC
☐ ○ Fiestas	So Fine	1958	FC
☐ ○ Fiestas	The Hobo's Prayer	1961	SC
☐ ○ Fireflies	I Can't Say Goodbye	1959	SC
☐ ○ Fireflies	You Were Mine	1959	SN

Fireflies

Five Chances

□○ Five Blue Notes	The Beat Of Our Hearts	1954	SP
□○ Five Chances	All I Want	1955	SP
□○ Five Chances	Gloria	1956	SC
□○ Five Crowns	Lullaby Of The Bells	1952	SP
□○ Five Crowns	You Came To Me	1955	SP

Five Crowns

Five Discs

□○ Five Discs	I Remember	1958	FC
□○ Five Discs	Adios	1961	FN
□○ Five Discs	My Baby Loves Me	1961	SN
□○ Five Discs	Never Let You Go	1961	FN
□○ Five Discs	That Was The Time	1962	SN
□○ Five Dollars	That's The Way It Goes	1960	SC

Five Dollars

Five Emeralds

□ ○ Five Embers	Please Come Home	1954	SP
□ ○ Five Emeralds	Darling	1954	SP
□ ○ Five Emeralds	I'll Beg	1954	SP
□ ○ Five Keys	Glory Of Love	1951	SP
□ ○ Five Keys	With A Broken Heart	1951	SP
□ ○ Five Keys	Red Sails In The Sunset	1952	SP

Five Keys

□ ○ Five Keys	These Foolish Things	1953	SP
□ ○ Five Keys	Deep In My Heart	1954	SP
□ ○ Five Keys	Ling Ting Tong	1954	FP
□ ○ Five Keys	Close Your Eyes	1955	SP
□ ○ Five Keys	I Wish I'd Never Learned	1955	SP

□ ○ Five Keys   The Verdict   1955   SP

□ ○ Five Keys   Out Of Sight, Out Of Mind   1956   SP

□ ○ Five Keys   Wisdom Of A Fool   1956   SP

□ ○ Five Notes   You Are So Beautiful   1955   SC

Five Notes

Five Royales

□ ○ Five Notes   Show Me The Way   1956   SC

□ ○ Five Royales   Give Me One More Chance   1951   SP

□ ○ Five Royales   My Wants For Love   1956   SP

□ ○ Five Royales   Dedicated To The One I Love   1957   SP

□ ○ Five Satins   I Remember (In The Still Of The Night)   1956   SC

□ ○ Five Satins   Wonderful Girl   1956   SC

□ ○ Five Satins   Oh Happy Day   1957   SC

□ ○ Five Satins   Our Anniversary   1957   SC

□ ○ Five Satins   To The Aisle   1957   SC

□ ○ Five Satins   Wishing Ring   1961   SN

Five Satins

Five Sharps

□ ○ Five Sharps	Stormy Weather	1952	SP
□ ○ Flairs	This Is The Night For Love	1954	SP
□ ○ Flairs (Cornel Gunter & the)	She Wants To Rock	1956	FC

Cornel Gunter & the Flairs

Flamingos

□ ○ Flamingos	Golden Teardrops	1953	SP
□ ○ Flamingos	If I Can't Have You	1953	SP
□ ○ Flamingos	Someday Someway	1953	FP
□ ○ Flamingos	Dream Of A Lifetime	1954	SP
□ ○ Flamingos	Jump Children	1954	FP
□ ○ Flamingos	A Kiss From Your Lips	1956	SP
□ ○ Flamingos	I'll Be Home	1956	SP
□ ○ Flamingos	Lovers Never Say Goodbye	1958	SC
□ ○ Flamingos	I Only Have Eyes For You	1959	SC

□ ○ Flamingos	Mio Amore	1960	SC
□ ○ Flamingos	Nobody Loves Me Like You Do	1960	FN
□ ○ Fleetwoods	Come Softly To Me	1959	MN

Fleetwoods   *Little Joey & the Flips*

□ ○ Fleetwoods	Mr. Blue	1959	MN
□ ○ Flips (Little Joey & the)	Bongo Stomp	1962	FN
□ ○ Four Bars	If I Give My Heart To You	1954	SP

Four Bars

Four Buddies

□ ○ Four Buddies	I Will Wait	1951	SP
□ ○ Four Buddies	Just To See You Smile Again	1951	SP
□ ○ Four Buddies	Simply Say Goodbye	1951	SP
□ ○ Four Buddies	Why At A Time Like This	1951	SP
□ ○ Four Buddies	You're Part Of Me	1952	SP
□ ○ Four Deuces	W-P-L-J	1955	FP

□○ Four Dots (Jerry Stone & the)	Pleading For Your Love	1959	SC
□○ Four Fellows	Angels Say	1955	SP
□○ Four Fellows	In The Rain	1955	SP
□○ Four Fellows	Soldier Boy	1955	SP
□○ Four Fellows	Darling You	1956	SP
□○ Four Fellows	You Don't Know Me	1956	SP
□○ Four Fellows	Give Me Back My Broken Heart	1957	SP

Four Fellows

Four Flames

□○ Four Flames	Tabarin	1951	SP
□○ Four Haven Knights	In My Lonely Room	1956	FC
□○ Four Haven Knights	Just To Be In Love	1957	SC

Four Haven Knights

Four J's

| □○ Four J's | Here I Am Broken Hearted | 1964 | FN |

| □ ○ G-Clefs | 'Cause You're Mine | 1956 | FC |
| □ ○ G-Clefs | Darla My Darling | 1956 | FC |

G-Clefs

Gems

□ ○ G-Clefs	Ka Ding Dong	1956	FC
□ ○ G-Clefs	Symbol Of Love	1957	SC
□ ○ Gardenias	Flaming Love	1956	FC
□ ○ Gay Knights	The Loudness Of My Heart	1958	SC
□ ○ Gaytunes	I Love You	1957	SC
□ ○ Gaytunes	Plea In The Moonlight	1958	FC
□ ○ Gazelles	Honest	1956	SC
□ ○ Gems	'Deed I Do	1954	SP
□ ○ Gems	You're Tired Of Love	1954	SP
□ ○ Genies	Who's That Knockin'	1959	FC

Genies

Gladiators

□○ Gentlemen	Don't Leave Me Baby	1954	FC
□○ Gladiators	Girl Of My Heart	1957	SC
□○ Gladiolas	Little Darlin'	1957	FC

Gladiolas

Guytones

□○ Globetrotters	Rainy Day Bells	1970	FC
□○ Goldentones	The Meaning Of Love	1955	SC
□○ Greco, Johnny (& group)	Rocket Ride	1963	FN
□○ Greene, Barbara (& group)	Long Tall Sally	1963	FN /FL
□○ Guytones	This Is Love	1957	FC
□○ Halos	Nag	1961	FN

Halos

Harmonaires

□○ Harmonaires	Come Back	1957	FC

□ ○ Harmonaires	Lorraine	1957	SC
□ ○ Harptones	A Sunday Kind Of Love	1953	SP
□ ○ Harptones	Life Is But A Dream	1954	SP
□ ○ Harptones	Loving A Girl Like You	1954	SP
□ ○ Harptones	My Memories Of You	1954	SP
□ ○ Harptones	Since I Fell For You	1954	SP
□ ○ Harptones	On Sunday Afternoon	1956	SP
□ ○ Harptones	That's The Way It Goes	1956	SP
□ ○ Harptones	Three Wishes	1956	SP
□ ○ Harptones	Cry Like I Cried	1957	SP
□ ○ Harptones	The Shrine Of St. Cecilia	1957	SP

Harptones   *Thurston Harris & the Sharps*

□ ○ Harris, Thurston (w/the Sharps)	Little Bitty Pretty One	1957	FC
□ ○ Heart Beats Quintet (aka Heartbeats)	Tormented	1955	SC
□ ○ Heartbeats	A Thousand Miles Away	1956	SC
□ ○ Heartbeats	Crazy For You	1956	SC

175

| □○ Heartbeats | Darling How Long | 1956 | SC |
| □○ Heartbeats | Oh Baby Don't | 1956 | FC |

Heartbeats

□○ Heartbeats	People Are Talking	1956	SC
□○ Heartbeats	Rock 'n' Rollin' 'n' Rhythm ' n' Blues-n'	1956	FC
□○ Heartbeats	Your Way	1956	SC
□○ Heartbeats	Down On My Knees	1958	SC
□○ Heartbreakers (A)	Heartbreaker	1951	SP

Heartbreakers (A)   *Heartbreakers (B)*

□○ Heartbreakers (B)	Without A Cause	1957	FC
□○ Hearts (A) (Lee Andrews & the)	Maybe You'll Be There	1954	SP
□○ Hearts (A) Lee Andrews & the)	Bluebird Of Happiness	1956	SP

□○ Hearts (A) Lee Andrews & the)	Lonely Room	1956	SC
□○ Hearts (A) Lee Andrews & the)	Long Lonely Nights	1957	SP
□○ Hearts (A) Lee Andrews & the)	Teardrops	1957	SP
□○ Hearts (A) Lee Andrews & the)	The Clock	1957	FC
□○ Hearts (A) Lee Andrews & the)	Try The Impossible	1958	SP
□○ Hearts (A) Lee Andrews & the)	Why Do I	1958	SP
□○ Hearts (A) Lee Andrews & the)	I'm Sorry Pillow	1963	SP

Lee Andrews & the Hearts (A)   *Hearts (B)*

□○ Hearts (B)	Lonely Nights	1955	SC /FG
□○ Hearts (B)	He Drives Me Crazy	1956	SC /FG
□○ Hemlocks (Little (Little Bobby Rivera &)	Cora Lee	1957	FC
□○ Hi-Fives	Dorothy	1958	FC

Hi-Fioves

Ronnie & the Hi-Lites (A)

☐○ Hi-Lites (A)   I Wish That We Were Married   1962   SN
     (Ronnie & the)

☐○ Hi-Lites (B)   Gloria   1962   SN

☐○ Hi-Lites (B)   Pretty Face   1962   SN

Hi-Lites (B)

Hollywood Flames

☐○ Hide-A-Ways   Can't Help Loving That Girl   1954   SP
                         Of Mine

☐○ Hits (Tiny Tim & the) Wedding Bells   1958   SC

☐○ Hollywood Flames   Peggy   1954   SP

☐○ Hollywood Flames   Buzz Buzz Buzz   1957   FC

☐○ Hollywood Flames   Just For You   1959   SC

☐○ Hornets   Crying Over You   1957   SC

☐○ Hurricanes   Dear Mother   1956   SC

□○ Hurricanes	Maybe It's All For The Best	1956	SC
□○ Hurricanes	Fallen Angel	1957	SC
□○ Hurricanes	Priceless	1957	SC

Hurricanes

Imaginations

□○ Imaginations	Hey You	1961	SN
□○ Imaginations	Mystery Of You	1961	FN
□○ Imaginations	The Search Is Over	1961	SN
□○ Impalas	Sorry (I Ran All The Way Home)	1959	FC

Impalas

Little Anthony & the Imperials (B)

□○ Imperials (A) SP	My Darling	1952	
□○ Imperials (B) (Little Anthony &)	So Much	1958	SC
□○ Imperials (B) (Little Anthony &)	Tears On My Pillow	1958	SC

□○ Imperials (B) (Little Anthony &)	Two People In The World	1958	SC
□○ Imperials (B) (Little Anthony &)	Shimmy, Shimmy Ko-Ko-Bop	1959	MC
□○ Imperials (B) (Little Anthony &)	When You Wish Upon A Star	1959	SC
□○ Imperials (B) (Little Anthony &)	Traveling Stranger	1961	FC
□○ Impressions (Jerry Butler & the)	For Your Precious Love	1958	SN

Ivy-Tones

Jerry Butler & the impressions

□○ Initials (Angelo & the)	Bells Of Joy	1959	SC
□○ Ivy-Tones	Oo-Wee Baby	1958	FC
□○ Jacks	Why Don't You Write Me	1955	SP
□○ Jacks	Why Did I Fall In Love	1956	SC

Jacks

Jaguars

□ ○ Jaguars	The Way You Look Tonight	1956	SP
□ ○ Jamies	Summertime, Summertime	1958	FC /FL

Jamies

Jayhawks

□ ○ Jayhawks	Stranded In The Jungle	1956	FC
□ ○ Jaytones	Oh Darling	1958	FC
□ ○ Jelly Beans	I Wanna Love Him So Bad	1964	FN /FG

Jelly Beans

Jesters

□ ○ Jesters	I'm Falling In Love	1957	FC
□ ○ Jesters	Love No One But You	1957	SC
□ ○ Jesters	Please Let Me Love You	1957	SC
□ ○ Jesters	So Strange	1957	SC

□ ○ Jesters	I Laughed	1958	FC
□ ○ Jesters	Now That You're Gone	1958	SC
□ ○ Jesters	Oh Baby	1958	FC
□ ○ Jesters	The Plea	1958	SC
□ ○ Jets	Heaven Above Me	1956	FC

Jewels

Jive Bombers

□ ○ Jewels	Hearts Of Stone	1954	FP
□ ○ Jive Bombers	Bad Boy	1957	SP
□ ○ Jive Five	My True Story	1961	SN
□ ○ Jive Five	Never, Never	1961	SN
□ ○ Jive Five	These Golden Rings	1962	SN
□ ○ Jive Five	What Time Is It	1962	SN

Jive Five

Herb Johnson (ctr.) & the Cruisers

□ ○ Johnson, Herb (bb/Cruisers)	Have You Heard	1960	MN

□ ○ Joytones	My Foolish Heart	1956	SC /FG

Joytones

Jimmy Castor & the Juniors

□ ○ Juniors (A) (Jimmy Castor &)	Somebody Mentioned Your Your Name	1957	SC
□ ○ Juniors (B) (Danny & the)	At The Hop	1957	FC
□ ○ Juniors (B) (Danny & the)	Rock And Roll Is Here To Stay	1957	FC
□ ○ Juniors (B) (Danny & the)	Sometimes When I'm All Alone	1957	SC

Danny & the Juniors

Kac-Ties

□ ○ Kac-Ties	Happy Birthday	1963	SC
□ ○ Keynotes	In The Evening	1956	FC
□ ○ Keynotes	Really Wish You Were Here	1956	FC
□ ○ Keynotes	One Little Kiss	1957	SC

Keynotes

Keystoners

□○ Keystoners	Sleep And Dream	1961	FC
□○ Keytones	Seven Wonders Of The World	1957	SC
□○ King Crooners	Now That She's Gone	1959	SC
□○ King Crooners	She's Mine All Mine	1959	FC
□○ King Crooners	Won't You Let Me Know	1959	FC
□○ Knockouts	Darling Lorraine	1959	SC

Kodaks

Knockouts

□○ Kodaks (aka Kodoks)	Little Boy And Girl	1957	FC /FL
□○ Kodaks (aka Kodoks)	Oh Gee, Oh Gosh	1957	FC /FL
□○ Kodaks (aka Kodoks)	Teenager' s Dream	1957	SC /FL

□○ Kodaks (aka Kodoks)	Runaround Baby	1960	FC /FL
□○ Kool Gents	This Is The Night	1956	SC

Kool Gents

Kuf-Linx

□○ Kuf-Linx	So Tough	1958	FC
□○ Ladders	Counting The Stars	1957	FC
□○ Laddins	Did It	1957	FC
□○ Laddins	Yes, Oh Baby Yes	1959	FC

Laddins

Lamplighters

□○ Lamplighters	I Used To Cry Mercy, Mercy	1954	FP
□○ Larks (A)	Hopefully Yours	1951	SP
□○ Larks (A)	My Reverie	1951	SP
□○ Larks (A)	Darlin'	1952	SP
□○ Larks (A)	In My Lonely Room	1952	SP

□○ Larks (A)   If It's A Crime   1954   SP

Larks (B) w/Don Julian

Larks (A)

□○ Larks (B) (w/   There Is A Girl   1961   FN
    Don Julian)

□○ Leaders   Stormy Weather   1955   SP

Curtis Lee bb/Halos

Leaders

□○ Lee, Curtis   Pretty Little Angel Eyes 1961   FN
    (bb/Halos)

□○ Legends   I'll Never Fall In Love Again   1957   FC

□○ Legends   The Legend Of Love   1958   SC

Joey & the Lexingtons

Lamplighters

□○ Lexingtons (Joey & the	Bobbie	1963	FN
□○ Limelighters	Cabin Hideaway	1956	FC
□○ Limelites (Shep & the)	Daddy's Home	1961	SC
□○ Limelites (Shep & the)	Our Anniversary	1962	SC
□○ Limelites (Shep & the)	Three Steps To The Altar	1962	SC

Shep & the Limelites

Love Notes

□○ Lollypops	Believe In Me	1958	FC
□○ Love Notes	Tonight	1957	FC
□○ Love Notes	United	1957	SC
□○ Ly-Dells	Wizard Of Love	1961	FN
□○ Lyrics	You And Your Fellow	1961	FN

Lydells

Lyric

| □○ Lytations | Look Into The Sky | 1964 | FC |

Lytations

Johnny Maestro

□○ Maestro, Johnny & group	What A Surprise	1961	SC
□○ Magnificent Four	The Closer You Are	1961	FN
□○ Magnificents	Up On The Mountain	1956	FP
□○ Magnificents	Don't Leave Me	1958	FC

Magnificents

Majors (B)

□○ Majestics	Nitey Nite	1956	SC
□○ Majors (A)	Laughing On The Outside, Crying On The Inside	1951	SP
□○ Majors (B)	A Wonderful Dream	1962	FN
□○ Marcels	Blue Moon	1961	FN
□○ Marcels	Goodbye To Love	1961	SN
□○ Marcels	Heartaches	1961	FN

Marcels

Marvelettes

□ ○ Marquis	Bohemian Daddy	1956	FC
□ ○ Marvelettes	Please Mr. Postman	1961	FN /FG
□ ○ Marvelettes	Forever	1963	SN /FG
□ ○ Marvelows	I Do	1965	FN

Marvelows

Marvels (aka Dubs)

□ ○ Marvels (aka Dubs)	I Won't Have You Breaking My Heart	1956	SC
□ ○ Marylanders	I'm A Sentimental Fool	1952	SP
□ ○ Marylanders	Make Me Thrill Again	1952	SP
□ ○ Master-Tones	Tell Me	1954	SP

Master-Tones

Rick & the Masters

□ ○ Masters (Rick   I Don't Want Your Love   1963   FN
      & the)

□ ○ Matadors   Vengeance (Will Be Mine)   1958   SC

□ ○ McFadden, Ruth   Two In Love   1956   SC
      (bb/Royaltones)   /FL

Ruth McFadden bb/Royaltones

Don Julian & the Meadowlarks

□ ○ Meadowlarks (Don Always And Always   1955   SP
      Julian & the)

□ ○ Meadowlarks (Don Heaven And Paradise   1955   SC
      Julian & the)

□ ○ Meadowlarks (Don This Must Be Paradise   1955   SC
      Julian & the)

□ ○ Medallions (Vernon Buick '59   1954   FP
      Green & the)

□ ○ Medallions (Vernon The Letter   1954   SP
      Green & the)

Mello-Harps

*Vernon Green &
the Medllions*

□ ○ Mello-Harps   Love Is A Vow   1955
      SC

□ ○ Mello-Kings   Tonight Tonight   1957   SC

Mello-Kings

Mello-Moods

□ ○ Mello-Moods	How Could You	1952	SP
□ ○ Mello-Moods	Where Are You? (Now That I Need You)	1952	SP
□ ○ Mellows (Lillian Leach & the)	How Sentimental Can I Be?	1954	SP /FL
□ ○ Mellows (Lillian Leach & the)	Smoke From Your Cigarette	1955	SP /FL
□ ○ Mellows (Lillian Leach & the)	Yesterday's Memories	1955	SP /FL
□ ○ Mellows (Lillian Leach & the)	My Darling	1956	SP /FL
□ ○ Mellows (Lillian Leach & the)	Moon Of Silver	1956	SP /FL

Lillian Leach & the Mellows

Metronomes

□ ○ Metronomes	I Love My Girl	1957	SC
□ ○ Midnighters (aka Royals)	Work With Me Annie	1953	FP
□ ○ Midnighters (aka Royals)	Sexy Ways	1954	FP
□ ○ Midnighters (aka Royals)	Partners For Life	1956	SC

Midnighters (aka Royals)

Moniques

□ ○ Monarchs	Always Be Faithful	1956	FC
□ ○ Monarchs	In My Younger Days	1956	FC
□ ○ Monarchs	Pretty Little Girl	1956	FC
□ ○ Moniques	All The Way Now	1963	FC
□ ○ Monotones	Book Of Love	1958	FC

Monotones

Moonglows

□ ○ Montclairs	Give Me A Chance	1956	SC
□ ○ Moonglows	Secret Love	1954	SP
□ ○ Moonglows	Sincerely	1954	SP
□ ○ Moonglows	In My Diary	1955	SP
□ ○ Moonglows	Most Of All	1955	SP
□ ○ Moonglows	Seesaw	1956	FP
□ ○ Moonglows	We Go Together	1956	SP
□ ○ Moonglows	When I'm With You	1956	SP
□ ○ Moonglows (Bobby Lester & the)	Penny Arcade	1962	SP
□ ○ Moonglows Lester & the)	Ten Commandments Of Love	1958	SC
□ ○ Mystics	Don't Take The Stars	1959	FC
□ ○ Mystics	Hushabye	1959	MC
□ ○ Mystics	All Through The Night	1960	SC
□ ○ Mystics	White Cliffs Of Dover	1960	FC

□○ Mystics Darling I Know Now 1961 FN

Mystics *Native Boys*

□○ Native Boys Strange Love 1956 FC

□○ Neons Angel Face 1956 FC

Neons *Nicky & the Nobles*

□○ New Yorkers 5 Gloria, My Darling 1955 SC

□○ Nobles (Nicky Poor Rock & Roll 1958 FC
   & the)

□○ Note-Torials My Valerie 1959 FC

Nutmegs

Note-Torials

Nutmegs

□ ○ Nutmegs	Ship Of Love	1955	SC
□ ○ Nutmegs	Story Untold	1955	SC
□ ○ Nutmegs	Whispering Sorrows	1955	SC
□ ○ Nutmegs	A Love So True	1956	SC
□ ○ Nutmegs	My Story	1959	SC
□ ○ Nutmegs	Down In Mexico	1963	FC
□ ○ Nutmegs	Down To Earth	1963	SC
□ ○ Nutmegs	Hello	1963	SC
□ ○ Nutmegs	Let Me Tell You	1963	FC
□ ○ Olympics	Western Movies	1958	FC
□ ○ Olympics	Dance By The Light Of The Moon	1960	FN

Olympics

Opals (aka Crystals)

□ ○ Opals (aka	Come To Me Darling	1954	SP

Crystals)

□○ Opals (aka Crystals)	My Heart's Desire	1954	SP
□○ Orchids	Newly Wed	1955	SC
□○ Orchids	You Said You Loved Me	1955	SC
□○ Orchids	You're Everything To Me	1955	SC
□○ Orients	Queen Of The Angels	1964	SN
□○ Orioles (Sonny Til & the)	It's Too Soon To Know	1948	SP
□○ Orioles (Sonny Til & the)	A Kiss And A Rose	1949	SP
□○ Orioles (Sonny Til & the)	Tell Me So	1949	SP
□○ Orioles (Sonny Til & the)	What Are You Doing New	1949	SP

Sonny Til & the Orioles

□○ Orioles (Sonny Til & the)	At Night	1950	SP
□○ Orioles (Sonny Til & the)	I'd Rather Have You Under The Moon	1950	SP

□ ○ Orioles (Sonny Til & the)   I Miss You So   1951   SP

□ ○ Orioles (Sonny Til & the)   Crying In The Chapel   1953   SP

□ ○ Orioles (Sonny Til & the)   I Cover The Waterfront   1953   SP

Packards

Darrell & the Oxfords

□ ○ Oxfords (Darrell & the)   Picture In My Wallet   1959   SN

□ ○ Packards   Dream Of Love   1956   SC

□ ○ Paradons   Diamonds And Pearls   1960   SN

Paradons

Paragons

□ ○ Paragons   Florence   1957   SC

□ ○ Paragons   Hey, Little School Girl   1957   FC

□ ○ Paragons   Let's Start All Over Again   1957   SC

□ ○ Paragons	Stick With Me Baby	1957	FC
□ ○ Paragons	So You Will Know	1958	SC
□ ○ Paragons	The Vows Of Love	1958	SC
□ ○ Paragons	Twilight	1958	SC

Passions

Pastels

□ ○ Passions	Just To Be With You	1959	SC
□ ○ Passions	I Only Want You	1960	FC
□ ○ Passions	This Is My Love	1960	SC
□ ○ Pastels	Been So Long	1958	SP
□ ○ Pastels	So Far Away	1958	SP

Pearls

Penguins

□ ○ Pearls	Let's You And I Go Steady	1956	FC

□○ Pearls	Your Cheating Heart	1957	FC
□○ Penguins	Earth Angel	1954	SP
□○ Penguins	Hey Senorita	1954	FP
□○ Penguins	My Troubles Are Not At End	1956	SC
□○ Penguins	Memories Of El Monte	1963	SN
□○ Pentagons	To Be Loved (Forever)	1960	SN

Pentagons

Personalities

□○ Perfections	Hey Girl	1959	FC
□○ Personalities	Woe Woe Baby	1957	FC
□○ Personalities	Yours To Command	1957	SC
□○ Phillips, Phil (w/ Twilights)	Sea Of Love	1959	SN

Phil Phillips

Gladys Knight & the Pips

□○ Pips (Gladys Knight & the)	Every Beat Of My Heart	1961	SC /FL

□○ Pixies Three	442 Glenwood Avenue	1963	FN /FG
□○ Pixies Three	Birthday Party	1963	FN /FG

Pixies Three   *Plants*

□○ Plants	Dear I Swear	1957	FC
□○ Platters	I'll Cry When You're Gone	1953	SP
□○ Platters	Voo-Vee-Ah-Bee	1954	FP
□○ Platters	Only You (And You Alone)	1955	SP
□○ Platters	The Great Pretender	1955	SP
□○ Platters	Heaven On Earth	1956	SP

Platters

□○ Platters	My Prayer	1956	SP
□○ Platters	On My Word Of Honor	1956	SP
□○ Platters	You'll Never Never Know	1956	SP

□ ○ Platters	(You've Got) The Magic Touch	1956	SP
□ ○ Platters	My Dream	1957	SP
□ ○ Platters	Smoke Gets In Your Eyes	1958	SP
□ ○ Platters	Twilight Time	1958	SP
□ ○ Poets	Vowels Of Love	1958	FC

Poni-Tails

Premiers (A)

□ ○ Poni-Tails	Born Too Late	1958	SC /FG
□ ○ Premiers (A)	My Darling	1956	SC
□ ○ Premiers (A)	Is This A Dream?	1957	SC
□ ○ Premiers (B) w/Herb Johnson	Help	1960	FC

Herb Johnson & the Premiers (B)

Prisonaires

□ ○ Prisonaires	Just Walkin' In The Rain	1953	SP
□ ○ Pyramids (A)	And I Need You	1955	SC

□ ○ Pyramids (B)	Ankle Bracelet	1958	SC
□ ○ Pyramids (B)	Hot Dog Dooly Wah	1958	FC
□ ○ Queens (Shirley Gunter & the)	Oop-Shoop	1954	FP /FG
□ ○ Queens (Shirley Gunter & the)	You're Mine	1955	FP /FG

Shirley Gunter & the Queens   *Quin-Tones*

□ ○ Quin-Tones	Down The Aisle Of Love	1958	SC /FL
□ ○ Quinns	Hong Kong	1958	FC
□ ○ Quinns	Oh Starlight	1958	SC

Quotations   *Rainbows (A)*

□ ○ Quotations	Ala-Men-Sa-Aye	1961	FN
□ ○ Quotations	Imagination	1961	FN

□○ Rainbows (A)	Mary Lee	1955	FC
□○ Rainbows (A)	Stay	1956	SC
□○ Rainbows (A)	They Say	1957	SC
□○ Rainbows (B) (Randy & the)	Denise	1963	FN
□○ Rainbows (B) (Randy & the)	She's My Angel	1963	FC

Randy & the Rainbows (B)

Raindrops (B)

□○ Raindrops (A)	(I Found) Heaven In Love	1956	SC
□○ Raindrops (B)	The Kind Of Boy You Can't Forget	1963	FN /FL
□○ Rajahs (aka Nutmegs)	Shifting Sands	1957	FC

Rajahs

Ramblers (A) (aka Kings)

□○ Ramblers (A) (aka Kings)	Vadunt-Un-Va-Da Song	1954	SP

□○ Ramblers (B)	Come On Back	1963	FC
□○ Ravels (Sheriff & the)	Shombalor	1959	FC
□○ Ravens	Lullabye	1946	SP
□○ Ravens	Once In A While	1948	SP
□○ Ravens	September Song	1948	SP

Ravens

□○ Ravens	Until The Real Thing Comes Along	1948	SP
□○ Ravens	Count Every Star	1950	SP
□○ Ravens	Time Takes Care Of Everything	1950	SP
□○ Ravens	You Foolish thing	1951	SP
□○ Ravens	Don't Mention My Name	1953	SP
□○ Rays	Silhouettes	1957	SC
□○ Re-Vels	False Alarm	1958	FC

Rays

Re-Vuela

□○ Reflections   (Just Like) Romeo And Juliet   1964   FN

Reflections

Tommy Regan

□○ Regan, Tommy   I'll Never Stop Loving You   1964   FN
    (bb/Marcels or Halos???)

□○ Regents   Barbara Ann   1961   FN

□○ Regents   Runaround   1961   FN

Regents

Riffs

□○ Revalons   Dreams Are For Fools   1958   FC

□○ Rialtos   Let Me In   1962   FN

| □○ Riffs | Little Girl | 1964 | FN |

| □○ Rivera, Lucy (& group) | Make Me Queen Again | 1959 | SN /FL |

Lucy Rivera (aka Lucy Cedeno)

Rivieras

□○ Rivieras	Count Every Star	1958	SN
□○ Rivieras	Moonlight Cocktails	1960	SC
□○ Rivileers	A Thousand Stars	1954	SP

Rivileers

Rivingtons

□○ Rivingtons	Papa Oom-Mow-Mow	1962	FN
□○ Rob Roys (Norman Fox & the)	Tell Me Why	1957	FC
□○ Rob Roys (Norman (Fox & the)	Dance Girl Dance	1958	FC
□○ Rob Roys (Norman (Fox & the)	Dream Girl	1958	FC
□○ Rob Roys (Norman	Pizza Pie	1958	FC

(Fox & the)

□ ○ Rob Roys (Norman   Lover Doll   1972   FC
        (Fox & the)

Norman Fox & the Rob Roys

Robins

□ ○ Robins   A Fool Such As I   1952   SP

□ ○ Robins   How Would You Know   1953   SP

□ ○ Robins   Smoky Joe's Cafe   1955   FP

Rocketones

Lenny Dean & the
Rockin' Chairs

□ ○ Rocketones   Dee I   1957   SC

□ ○ Rocketones   Mexico   1957   FC

□ ○ Rockin' Chairs   A Kiss Is A Kiss   1959   FC
        (Lenny Dean &)

□ ○ Rockin' Chairs   Memories Of Love   1959   FC
        (Lenny Dean &)

□ ○ Rockin' Chairs   Please Mary Lou   1959   FC
        (Lenny Dean &)

□ ○ Romans (Little   Those Oldies But Goodies   1961   SN
    Caesar & the)   (Remind Me Of You)

Little Caesar & the Romans

Roomates

□ ○ Roomates   Band Of Gold   1961   SN

□ ○ Roomates (Cathy   Please Love Me Forever   1960   SN
    Jean & the)   /FL

Cathy Jean

Rosebuds

□ ○ Rosebuds   Dearest Darling   1957   SC
                                                  /FG

Roulettes

Royal Teens

□ ○ Roulettes   I See A Star   1958   SC

□ ○ Royal Teens	Believe Me	1959	FC
□ ○ Royals (A) (aka Midnighters)	A Love Of My Heart	1952	SP
□ ○ Royals (A) (aka Midnighters)	Every Beat Of My Heart	1952	SP
□ ○ Royals (A) (aka Midnighters)	Moonrise	1952	SP
□ ○ Royals (A) (aka Midnighters)	Starting From Tonight	1952	SP

Royals (A) (aka Midnighters)

Richie & the Royals (B)

□ ○ Royals (B) Richie & the)	And When I'm Near You	1961	FN
□ ○ Royaltones	Crazy Love	1956	FC
□ ○ Safaris	Image Of A Girl	1960	SC

Royaltones

Safaris

□ ○ Salutations (Vito & the)	Unchained Melody	1963	FN

Scarlets

Vito & the Salutations

□○ Scarlets	Dear One	1954	SP
□○ Scarlets	Love Doll	1955	SC
□○ Schoolboys	Please Say You Want Me	1957	SC
□○ Schoolboys	Shirley	1957	FC
□○ Schoolboys	Angel Of Love	1958	SC

Schoolboys

Scott Brothers

□○ Scott Brothers	Part Of You	1959	FC
□○ Selections	Guardian Angel	1958	FC
□○ Senors	May I Have This Dance	1962	MN
□○ Sensations	Please Mr. Disc Jockey	1956	SP /FL
□○ Sensations	My Debut To Love	1957	SP /FL
□○ Sensations	Let Me In	1961	FN

Sensations

Shells

□ ○ Serenaders	I Wrote A Letter	1957	FC
□ ○ Sharps	Love Me My Darling	1954	SP
□ ○ Shells	Baby Oh Baby	1957	SC
□ ○ Shells	What's In An Angel's Eyes	1957	SC
□ ○ Shells	Sippin' Soda	1958	SC

Shepherd Sisters

□ ○ Shepherd Sisters	Alone	1957	FC /FG
□ ○ Sheppards (A)	Sherry	1956	SC

Sheppards (A)

Sheppards (B)

□ ○ Sheppards (B)	Island Of Love	1959	SC
□ ○ Shields	You Cheated	1958	SC

Shields

Shirelles

□ ○ Shirelles	I Met Him On A Sunday	1958	FC /FG
□ ○ Shirelles	Dedicated To The One I Love	1959	SN /FG
□ ○ Shirelles	Tonight's The Night	1960	MN
□ ○ Shirelles	Will You Love Me Tomorrow	1960	MN /FG
□ ○ Shirelles	Baby It's You	1961	SN /FG
□ ○ Shirelles	Mama Said	1961	FN /FG
□ ○ Shirelles	Soldier Boy	1962	SN /FG
□ ○ Showmen	It Will Stand	1961	FN

Showmen

Silhouettes

□ ○ Silhouettes	Get A Job	1957	FC
□ ○ Silhouettes	Bing Bong	1958	FC
□ ○ Silhouettes	I Sold My Heart To The Junkman	1958	SC
□ ○ Sinceres	Please Don't Cheat On Me	1961	FN
□ ○ Six Teens	A Casual Look	1956	SC /FL

Six Teens

Skyliners

□ ○ Skarlettones	Do You Remember	1959	FC
□ ○ Skyliners	It Happened Today	1959	FC
□ ○ Skyliners	Lonely Way	1959	FC
□ ○ Skyliners	Since I Don't Have You	1959	SN
□ ○ Skyliners	This I Swear	1959	SN
□ ○ Skyliners	Pennies From Heaven	1960	FC
□ ○ Solitaires	Blue Valentine	1954	SC
□ ○ Solitaires	Please Remember My Heart	1954	SC
□ ○ Solitaires	South Of The Border	1954	MC
□ ○ Solitaires	Wonder Why	1954	SC

□ ○ Solitaires	I Don't Stand A Ghost Of A Chance	1955	SC

Solitaires

□ ○ Solitaires	Later For You Baby	1955	FC
□ ○ Solitaires	Nothing Like A Little Love	1956	SC
□ ○ Solitaires	The Angels Sang	1956	SC
□ ○ Solitaires	You've Sinned	1956	SC
□ ○ Solitaires	I Really Love You So (Honey Babe)	1957	FC
□ ○ Solitaires	Walkin' Along	1957	FC
□ ○ Sophomores (Anthony & the)	Embraceable You	1963	SC
□ ○ Sophomores (Anthony & the)	Play Those Oldies Mr. D.J.	1963	FN

Anthony & the Sophomores

Souvenirs

□ ○ Souvenirs	Double Dealing Baby	1957	FP
□ ○ Spaniels	Baby It's You	1953	SP
□ ○ Spaniels	The Bells Ring Out	1953	SP
□ ○ Spaniels	Goodnite Sweetheart Goodnite	1953	SP
□ ○ Spaniels	Let's Make Up	1954	SC

Spaniels

□ ○ Spaniels	You Painted Pictures	1955	SC
□ ○ Spaniels	You Gave Me Peace Of Mind	1956	SC
□ ○ Spaniels	Everyone's Laughing	1957	MC
□ ○ Spaniels	Stormy Weather	1958	FC
□ ○ Spectors Three	I Really Do	1960	MN

Spectors Three

Spiders

□ ○ Spiders	I Didn't Want To Do It	1954	FP
□ ○ Spiders	I'm Slippin' In	1954	FP
□ ○ Spiders	Love's All I'm Puttin' Down (rel. 1992)	1954	FP
□ ○ Spiders	Witchcraft	1955	FP
□ ○ Spiders	That's My Desire	1957	SP
□ ○ Spinners (Claudine Clark & the)	Party Lights	1962	FN /FL

Claudine Clark

Squires

| □ ○ Squires | Dreamy Eyes | 1957 | SC |
| □ ○ Starlites (A) | Missing You | 1957 | SC |

Starlites (A)

Eddie & the Starlites (B)

Jackie & the Starlites (C)

□○ Starlites (B) (Eddie   To Make A Long Story Short   1959   SC
   & the)

□○] Starlites (B) (Eddie   Come On Home   1963   SN
   & the)

□○ Starlites (C) (Jackie   Valerie   1960   SC
   & the)

□○ Stereos   I Really Love You   1961   FN

Stereos

Strangers

□○ Strangers   Blue Flowers   1954   SP

□○ Strangers   Hoping You'll Understand   1954   SP

□○ Strangers   My Friends   1954   SP

□○ Students   Every Day Of The Week   1958   FC

□○ Students   I'm So Young   1958   SC

Students

Sunbeams

□○ Summits   Go Back Where You Came   1961   FN

□ ○ Sunbeams	Come Please Say You'll Be Mine	1957	SC
□ ○ Superiors	Lost Love	1957	SC

Superiors

Supremes (C)

□ ○ Supremes (A)	Could This Be You	1956	SP
□ ○ Supremes (B) (Ruth McFadden & the)	Darling, Listen To The Words Of This Song	1956	SP /FL
□ ○ Supremes (C)	Just For You And I	1957	SC
□ ○ Swallows	Dearest	1951	SP
□ ○ Swallows	Eternally	1951	SP
□ ○ Swallows	It Ain't The Meat	1951	FP
□ ○ Swallows	Since You've Been Away	1951	SP
□ ○ Swallows	Will You Be Mine	1951	SP

Swallows

Swinging Hearts

□ ○ Swallows	Beside You	1952	SP
□ ○ Swallows	Please Baby Please	1952	MP
□ ○ Swans	My True Love	1953	SP
□ ○ Swinging Hearts	How Can I Love You	1961	SN
□ ○ Teardrops	The Stars Are Out Tonight	1954	SC

Techniques

Teddy Bears

□ ○ Techniques	Hey! Little Girl	1957	SC
□ ○ Teddy Bears	To Know Him Is To Love Him	1957	SC /FL
□ ○ Teenagers (Frankie Lymon & the)	ABCs Of Love	1956	FC
□ ○ Teenagers (Frankie Lymon & the)	I Promise To Remember	1956	FC
□ ○ Teenagers (Frankie Lymon & the)	I Want You To Be My Girl	1956	FC
□ ○ Teenagers (Frankie Lymon & the)	I'm Not A Know It All	1956	SC
□ ○ Teenagers (Frankie Lymon & the)	Share	1956	SC
□ ○ Teenagers (Frankie Lymon & the)	Why Do Fools Fall In Love	1956	FC
□ ○ Teenagers (Frankie Lymon & the)	Out In The Cold Again	1957	SC

☐○ Teenagers (Frankie Lymon & the)	Paper Castles	1957	FC
☐○ Teenagers (Frankie Lymon & the)	Teenage Love	1957	FC

Frankie Lymon & the Teenagers

☐○ Teenchords (Lewis Lymon & the)	Honey Honey	1957	FC
☐○ Teenchords (Lewis Lymon & the)	I'm Not Too Young To Fall	1957	FC
☐○ Teenchords (Lewis Lymon & the)	I'm So Happy (Tra-La-La-La)	1957	FC
☐○ Teenchords (Lewis Lymon & the)	Please Tell The Angels	1957	SC
☐○ Teenchords (Lewis Lymon & the)	Your Last Chance	1957	FC

Lewis Lymon & the Teenchords

□○ Tempo-Tones   So They Say   1957   SC
    (Nancy Lee &)   /FL

□○ Tempo-Tones (w/   Get Yourself Another Fool   1957   SC
    Richard Lanham)

Richard Lanham

Temptations (A)

□○ Temptations (A)   Standing Alone   1958   FC

□○ Temptations (B)   Barbara   1960   FC

Temptations (B)    *Three Chuckles*

□○ Three Chuckles   Runaround   1954   SP
    (w/Teddy Randazzo)

□○ Three Chuckles   Foolishly   1955   SP

□○ Three Friends   Blanche   1956   SC

Three Friends

Little Joe & the Thrillers

□ ○ Thrillers (Little Joe & the)	Peanuts	1957	FC
□ ○ Timetones (aka Time-Tones)	I've Got A Feeling	1961	SN
□ ○ Timetones (aka Time-Tones)	In My Heart	1961	FC
□ ○ Timetones (aka Time-Tones)	Pretty Pretty Girl (The New Beat)	1961	FC

Timetones (aka Time-Tones)

Tokens (B)

□ ○ Tokens (A)	Doom Lang	1957	FC
□ ○ Tokens (B)	The Lion Sleeps Tonight	1961	MN
□ ○ Tokens (B)	Tonight I Fell In Love	1961	FN
□ ○ Tonettes	Oh What A Baby	1958	FC /FG

Tonettes

Little Jimmy Rivers & the Tops

□○ Tops (Little Jimmy Rivers & the)	Puppy Love	1961	FC
□○ Treble Chords	Theresa	1959	FC
□○ Tremaines	Jingle Jingle	1958	FC
□○ Triumphs, Tico & the)	Cards Of Love	1963	FN

Tico & the
Triumphs

Tune Weavers

□○ Tru-Tones	Magic	1957	FC
□○ Tune Weavers	Happy Happy Birthday Baby	1957	SC /FL
□○ Turbans	When You Dance	1955	FC
□○ Turbans	Congratulations	1957	SC
□○ Turbans	Valley Of Love	1957	SC

Turbans

Turks

□○ Turks	Emily	1955	SP
□○ Tuxedos	Yes It's True	1960	SC

□ ○ Twilighters	Little Did I Dream	1955	SP
□ ○ Tymes	So Much In Love	1963	MN
□ ○ Tymes	Somewhere	1963	SN

Tymes

Universals

□ ○ Tyson, Roy (& group)	Oh What A Night For Love	1963	FC
□ ○ Uniques	Do You Remember	1959	SN
□ ○ Universals	A Love Only You Can Give	1962	SC
□ ○ Utopians (Mike & the)	Erlene	1958	FC
□ ○ Vacels (Ricky & the)	Lorraine	1962	SN

Ricky & the Vacels

Valentines

□ ○ Val-Chords	Candy Store Love	1957	FC
□ ○ Valentines	Lily Maebelle	1955	FC
□ ○ Valentines	Woo Woo Train	1955	FC
□ ○ Valentines	Nature's Creation	1956	SC
□ ○ Valentines	Don't Say Goodnight	1957	SC
□ ○ Valiants	This Is The Night	1957	SC

Valiants

Valrays

□ ○ Valrays	Yo Me Pregunto	1963	FN
□ ○ Van Dykes	Come On, Baby	1958	SC
□ ○ Vanguards	Moonlight	1958	SC
□ ○ Vel-Tones	Now	1960	FC
□ ○ Velours	My Love Come Back	1956	SC
□ ○ Velours	Can I Come Over Tonight	1957	SC
□ ○ Velours	This Could Be The Night	1957	SC
□ ○ Velvetones	The Glory Of Love	1957	SC
□ ○ Velvets (A)	I	1953	SP

| □○ Velvets (B) | Tonight (Could Be The Night) | 1961 | FN |

Velours

Velvetones

□○ Videls	Be My Girl	1959	FN
□○ Videls	Mr. Lonely	1960	MN
□○ Videos	Trickle Trickle	1958	FC

Velvets (B)

Videls

Videos

Viscaynes

□ ○ Viscaynes	Stop What You're Doing	1961	SC
□ ○ Vocaleers	Be True	1952	SP
□ ○ Vocaleers	It Is A Dream	1952	SP
□ ○ Vocaleers	I Walk Alone	1953	SP
□ ○ Voices	Two Things I Love	1955	FP
□ ○ Volumes	I Love You	1962	FN

Vocaleers

Voices

□ ○ Voxpoppers   Wishing For Your Love   1958   SC

Volumes

Voxpopper

□ ○ Wanderers   Thinking Of You   1957   SC

Wheels

Wanderers

□○ Wheels	My Heart's Desire	1956	SC
□○ Whirlers	Magic Mirror	1956	SC
□○ Whispers	Fool Heart	1954	SP

Whirlers

Whispers

□○ Willows	Church Bells May Ring	1956	FC
□○ Wrens	Beggin' For Love	1955	SP
□○ Wrens	Come Back My Love	1955	FP
□○ Wrens	C'est La Vie	1956	SC

Wrens

Youngsters

| □○ Youngsters | Shattered Dreams | 1956 | FC |

□ ○ Zodiacs (Maurice   Stay   1960   FC
        Williams & the)

Maurice
Williams &
the Zodiacs

Notes on the Top 1000

There are approximately 500 different groups appearing in the Top 1000. Almost 400 of these have pictures representing them in the above list, and the groups pictured sang over 850 of the Top 1000 songs. (This is because the more popular groups sang multiple songs.)

If the reader is interested in finding more information about the various groups and songs, we recommend two sources. Marv Goldberg has documented the careers of many of the above groups in his "R & B Notebooks" at http://www.uncamarvy.com/index.html. From that site, one can read about the groups and listen to hundreds of radio shows, put together by Goldberg.

The second is a series of fanzines put together by J. P. Marion, called "Doo- Wop Nation." Start at http://home.earthlink.net/%7Ejaymar41/index.html and click on "Doo-Wop Nation" to view his many articles.

As for the pictures found interspersed among the Top 1000, they were copied from various sources on the web. The most consistently helpful resource is found at: http://www.blogg.org/blog-65325-themes-_calvanes-171394.html. Put the name of a group in the search engine and it is likely to come up with a picture, a discography and information about the group and its members. Another approach is to put the name of the group into Google (adding "doo-wop" if the name is common, such as the Rays) and then clicking on "Images" at the top of the returned page.

For a comprehensive view of the genre, the best resource is still "The Complete Book of Doo-Wop," by Gribin and Schiff, available at Oldies.com. There are better sources for information on the groups themselves (e.g. Goldberg, Marion) but no other book covers the politics, geography and evolution of the genre better.

Postscript: HELP WANTED!

Although putting together this book was a labor of love and a thoroughly joyful experience, there is one thing that caused us pain. Namely, the need to limit our choices to 1000 songs. Selections had to be made and many worthwhile tracks didn't make the cut. There are several reasons.

One is the previously admitted (but unapologetic) biases that affect these authors, who are both New York City born and raised. We hope that these were somewhat lessened by exposure to both the mainstream doo-wop of Don K. Reed and the purist body of vocal group harmony championed by the late Ronnie Italiano and U.GH.A. In addition, our reaching out to experts from other parts of the country (Philadelphia, D.C./Baltimore, Chicago, Los Angeles and Southern music) also widened our knowledge and preferences.

A second factor was our decision to limit the number of songs by any one group. The Clyde McPhatter Drifters had many more songs that might have made the list, but at some point we felt a need to say "no mas." If we had drilled deeper into their music, there would have been less room on the list for less well-known groups and songs, as well as the occasional one-off good song by an unknown group.

Examples are "I'll Never Tell" and "My Success (It All Depends On You)" by the Harptones, "One Hundred Years From Today," "These Three Words" and "I Know, I Know" by the Spaniels, and "Summertime," "Sunday Kind Of Love," "One Last Kiss," and "Crazy Bells In My Heart" by the Marcels. Nine great songs that didn't make the cut.

Also left out were some non-mainstream songs such as "Harmony Of Love" by the Five Dollars, in which the bass part repeats "Bayou-di bompity boom" throughout the song with a falsetto lead ulelating above. The result is strange, yet haunting. A second tune is "That's All I Want From You (Chi-Wah-Wah)" by the Silva-Tones. "Chi Wah Wah" is in the title because it is murmured under the lead for the whole song. Then there's "Roaches Rock" by the Temptations, giving us a great bass lead and humorous lyrics. And "Zup Zup" by the Keynotes, a New York style ditty that starts out as a mid-tempo doo-wop and changes gears in the middle of the song. We wish we had room for all of them.

Further, we realize that other lovers of the music grew up with their own favorites that we have no way of divining. Or some alternate versions of the songs we've chosen performed by other groups. For example, everyone knows and most love the Harptones 1953 version of "Sunday Kind Of Love." Most will also know the uptempo version done by the Dell-Vikings in 1957. But there are plenty of others, including great versions by the Kings (1953), Marcels (1961) and Timetones (1963).

So this is where we put up our "HELP WANTED" sign. We'd like to hear from other lovers of this genre. Please e-mail any and all alternative tracks that you think should be included...in...tada... the Top Second 1000 tracks! We'll get to work as soon as we begin to hear from you. We can be reached at ajgribin@optonline.net.

www.ingramcontent.com/pod-product-compliance
Lightning Source LLC
Chambersburg PA
CBHW031834090426
42741CB00005B/242